The Mental Game of Golf

D Vardy

CASTLE
publications

Castle Publications
A Division of Nottingham University Press
Manor Farm, Main Street
Thrumpton, Nottingham, NG11 0AX, UK

NOTTINGHAM

First published 1996
© D Vardy

British Library Cataloguing in Publication Data
A catalogue record for this book is available from the British Library

ISBN 1-897676-581

Typeset by Castle Publications, Nottingham
Printed and bound by Redwood Books, Trowbridge, Wiltshire

PREFACE

It was as far back as the mid 1970's when I first became interested in the Mental Game of Golf. The time when I changed from being the Match Secretary of my golf club to take on the responsibility of organising the newly formed Junior Section.

My first project was to organise a suitable junior programme, but it seemed to have a missing link. I could arrange special teaching sessions and arrange competitions and matches, but how could I explain the importance of etiquette and how this affects performance?

My position in the Department of Psychology at the University of Nottingham was a distinct advantage. I was able to question different psychologists on the subject of stress management, and how emotion and performance are connected. I also decided to follow the Professional Tour, as often as time would allow, and see how the top players went about their business.

My book endeavours to explain the mental game in the language of golf with quotes, instances and occasions which hopefully, all golfers can relate to. Understanding the mental side of golf should help all golfers to enjoy their golf and improve their appreciation of this wonderful game.

ABOUT THE AUTHOR

Dennis Vardy started work on the Mental Game of Golf some 20 years ago and his research was run along two fronts. One to look at what the psychologist had to say and, just as importantly, to discuss mental game problems with professional golfers. Anger, fear and depression seemed to be part of playing golf, but how did this interfere with performance levels? Was it good to let off steam? And so on.

He has explained mental game theories to many golfers over the years and, in exchange, they have taught him their ways of dealing with the pressures of tour golf. Brian Waites and Andrew Murray particularly, have made a very significant input to his research and it is through the knowledge he gained from them, and others of course, that he has been able to write this book.

His first series of mental game articles was published in 1986 by Golf Illustrated and since then there have been articles published in Todays' Golfer, Golfers' Companion, Golf Weekly, Golf Monthly and a chapter in the book "Golf the Scientific Way."

Over the years he has worked with professionals, top amateurs and county squads, but being invited to coach the British Ladies Elite Squad was an important step forward for him. Along with Bernard Gallacher he worked with them for three years, during which time they won the Commonwealth Championships for the first time in 16 years and the Curtis Cup.

He is an invited lecturer and course organiser for the PGA of Great Britain and Ireland whose National Academy is based at the Belfry. He has developed and delivered 'Continued Professional Education' courses for qualified PGA members.

In his own words, "When I first started my research I thought that some of it may be difficult to understand and therefore difficult to explain - this has proved not to be so. The mental game of golf is easy to understand and consists mainly of a lot of common sense."

CONTENTS

Photographs courtesy of Today's Golfer Magazine and Sports Technology and Research Ltd

The difference between players like Severiano Ballesteros and Nick Faldo and the high handicap golfer is too wide to be related solely to the physical side of golf. It is the opinion of many golf thinkers that this gap could be dramatically reduced if all golfers spent a little of their time considering the mental aspects of golf. **(Figure 1 & 2)**

Figures 1 & 2: Seve and Nick

The Mental Game is nothing new, it's been around since golf began. But it is only in recent years that it has been studied and used as a teaching aid, and some golfers have been confused as to its usefulness. Sometimes they question its need, often without listening, and say that physical swing training is their only way forward. If this is so, why is it that some golfers cannot cope with competition golf? The simple answer is that golf is a personal challenge and this places the golfer under pressure. Everyone knows that long medal rounds are the result of the need to play well, and how this can dramatically interfere with the way they play. Understanding how to deal with pressure golf is the reason why all golfers should study the mental game of golf.

Champions have always been separated from others by the way they think. When the pressure of competition is on, some golfers can think clearly and play controlled positive golf - they are the champions. Bernhard Langer is a great example and always seems to be in personal control. He also portrays another quality which the game of golf deserves - he behaves like a gentleman at all times.

If you follow the PGA European Tour you can watch the players perform both on the course and on the practise areas. When practising they each hit the ball very much the same. Some even look the same, but when these players get out on the course, only a very few have any chance of winning. There has to be a reason for this and you could say they lack experience; but what is experience, is it a knowledge of the mental game?

Brian Waites once told me that at the height of his career he always felt that he was in competition with only a few other players. This was because the others rarely featured in the top ten. He said that when a golfer gets into a winning position he or she must know how to handle that position. If they can't then they will be back in the pack.

All golfers should take a serious look into why they play the game. Is it because golf is such a complex game? Is it for the comradeship? Is it for the competitiveness? Or is it simply for a walk in the fresh air? Most golfers will quote many reasons, but generally they say that above all they play to win. Unfortunately for many of them nothing other than winning seems to matter, and perhaps this is why there are so many grumpy players about. They put themselves under so much "pressure by demand" that they have no chance of realising their ambition.

The overwhelming urge to win can do strange things to people. It can make them criticise their performance to a level of being angry and then humiliate themselves by a show of nasty temper. Anger is created by either bad luck, bad shot, or bad lie, and it shows as bad temper. On the other hand, some golfers may be so determined to do well that they try too hard. They adopt an attitude which can create so much doubt and enquiry that getting down to actually play a shot takes an age. Sometimes the enquiry is still going on after the address position has been taken up and the resulting shot is almost certain to end in failure.

Golf can be an infuriating game and the need for self control is perhaps more important than in any other sport. The golfer has to exercise tolerance and patience both towards other people and himself. To remain in personal control is a basic requirement.

One way to seek the correct mood in which to play golf is through accepting the game as an interesting challenge. Golfers should see themselves being challenged by the course architect to play their way around a layout armed with the personal talent they have available. They should find interest in the chess type moves needed to conquer the course and see themselves being able to do this better than any one else. But the ultimate challenge they must see is the challenge within themselves. If they lose their self control through either anger or fear then failure will be the result. **(Figure 3)**

Golf is a complex game which needs a very fine order of coordination and timing. Together with being in control emotionally, there is an obvious need to be in control of the swing. We also need

Figure 3: View across the water towards the 18th green at the Belfry. This challenge has tested the best golfers in the world

to keep reminding ourselves of how to play and this we must do through regular practise sessions. Top golfers practise every day to keep their game together, and even then, they have to be very careful. They know that they must not change anything, just keep on grooving the same swing pattern - the same rhythm and timing in their quest for consistency. Practise at golf must be positive, it is so easy to practise bad technique both in the physical and the mental sense. Whatever we practise we will become good at it, be it good method or bad.

Unfortunately many golfers do not practise in a correct and positive manner. They spend hour after hour looking for something new - something which will transform their swing into the ultimate swing. A swing which will look good, produce good results under pressure and make them number one. But can this be achieved by constantly changing the swing? We see so many golfers hitting buckets of balls for hours on end expecting a game of golf to jump out and present itself to them. Golfers must understand positive practise.

Golf is a game of feelings, feelings that are generated within one's own mind. We all understand them - feelings of fear, feelings of anger and at the other extreme, feelings of joy and satisfaction. When everything is going well, the world is a wonderful place. We feel good, ooze confidence and we should try to remember these feelings. When the pressure is on, these are the feelings we must recall; if we don't or can't, then we have the recipe for gloom and failure.

A good understanding of the mental game will enable the golfer to know how to practise and be able to answer questions such as, "If I asked you to concentrate, what would you do?" "If I asked you to go out and play positive golf, what would you do?" "If I asked you to relax, what would you do?" There are many more questions and very simple ways to explain them. Golf is an interesting game and if you want to win, you must know how to handle the pressure.

CONCENTRATION

Even if you do have a classical swing, you will need to be able to "produce it on the day" as they say. **(Figure 4)**

Figure 4: Constantino Rocca has a great swing. He will always be remembered for this picture taken at The Open in 1995

There are perhaps more mental hazards at golf than there are physical ones and the need to avoid these is a most important part of learning to play golf. If you cannot control your emotions, you will not play good golf and may find it very difficult to find playing partners.

There are "set rules" to grip and to swing; there are also set rules on how to behave. Not just in the sense of being properly mannered - this should never be open to question - we should learn how our thinking processes should be organised. When playing golf we must know what to think about and when to think about it. Golf will then be more of the pleasure for which it was surely designed.

It has often been said in golfing circles that having the ability to concentrate is what makes the champion and this, though true, is true only to a certain extent because obviously other factors are involved.

To define concentration or attention, as psychologists would call it, one only needs to enlarge on the dictionary definition. The dictionary says "To employ one's full thoughts and effort". This means that at golf we must attend fully to every drive, chip or putt. It does not mean we must "think golf" all the time we are out at play. Trying to concentrate on just golf would be disastrous as I will explain later.

There are times when we find concentrating difficult and this is because "things" interfere; things like anger, fear, anxiety, noise, cold, wind and many more. Times when our conscious mind becomes so confused it goes a complete blank. It is incapable of coping with all the information we offer it and unable to give clear instructions.

We must therefore train our conscious minds to think more clearly and reduce the confusion. If we don't, then there will be times when

Notes

the pressure is on when we will be unable to instruct ourselves on the next move.

Do you remember the time when you played a long putt or chip and you were unbelievably short - so short it was laughable? Your mind was so taken up by examining the line, the left or right movement, loose impediments etc., you were unable to make the decision about just how hard to hit the ball.

Incidentally these "lapses" introduce other problems. What about those famous "yips" that have destroyed golfers of all abilities. They got Ben Hogan eventually and Peter Alliss gave up competitive golf for the same reasons. Peter has now moved on to a more successful career as a commentator. His informed comment is greatly admired throughout the golfing world and maybe we should thank his putting problems for bringing him into commentating earlier than he normally would have. **(Figure 5)**

Figure 5: Peter Alliss uses his knowledge of golf to be one of today's top golf commentators

For those who do not understand what it is like to yip, think yourselves very fortunate. Some golfers refer to it as a disease and it is brought about by remaining in a stationary position for too long a period of time. When golfers are considering a shot, particularly the pressure putt, they often hang around too long. Too much fear, too much thinking, too much indecision, all in a stationary position, arrive at the "freeze" and then the yip; an uncontrolled attempt to hit the ball.

We must decide therefore how to organise this time period more effectively. Whilst weighing up the putt, or any shot for that matter, keep on the move and do not take too long about it. One solution which should be tried by all those who have the tendency to yip is to start the putt by first releasing their grip on the putter to a level only just greater than letting go of it, then the backswing will be much easier. The backswing can then be achieved without a jerking motion.

Keep it simple and concentration at golf is so much easier. Relaxation obviously helps but we will provide ourselves with concentration if we engage in a method of pre-shot thoughts to lead into the swing. Learning to develop a swing sequence or set of "concentration steps" to use on each and every occasion will provide us with the concentration that many golfers find difficult.

Many learning processes involve watching and imitating and in golf this should be more widely used. When studying concentration methods it would help to watch how Bernhard Langer goes about his business. Bernhard has never been a "flash in the pan" champion; he will be around for as long as he wishes. He has all the attributes of the great champion. Very few have his ability to concentrate, be totally at peace with himself, and be able to shrug off the problems which could interfere with his game. **(Figure 6)**

Our ability to concentrate is only as good as our ability to avoid distraction. There will be times when you will be dominated by thoughts which are not relevant to golf. There are also those times when golf itself will present thoughts to distract us from what we are trying to do. Both of these can come under the heading of stress.

Figure 6:
Bernhard Langer
is always at peace
with himself

STRESS AT GOLF

The interference factors at golf are not just found during play. Their origins may lie miles away in the other parts of your life.

Very often these "emotional" distractions will dominate the mind to such a large extent and then become the only thoughts your mind will consider. The worry brought about by a relative or friend, a problem at business or just one of those silly arguments we have at home, usually about things not worth arguing about, may all make the "golf mind" difficult to organise.

To the professional, these problems, particularly the business ones, can be a major source of distraction. They are one reason why some players rise and fall very quickly. It can be quite difficult for the professional, and the amateur for that matter, to forget his off-course business and switch into his "golf world". A lack of ability to cope with the business side of his profession should lead the professional to employ a good manager; a person who will relieve the burden and take on the responsibility of off-course interference. This will leave a more peaceful time for him to attend to what he is good at - playing the game.

Top golfers can have many commitments other than playing and too much will affect their play. We all find that life often presents us with things we do not like to do, such as going to the dentist, so adding other likes or dislikes can overload our minds and chip away at our powers of attention. Everyone has a workload limit and we should ensure this limit is never reached and do not forget, you can over-work just as easily doing things you like doing. It does not have to be uninteresting work, everyone must rest in order to recharge their batteries. Work under-load is another problem which needs to be considered.

Boredom is itself a problem and is a contributing factor in lost concentration. This can attack the golfer both on and off the course, so for all professionals filling the gaps and changing the scene is also work for the manager. And if the manager does not understand the mental game then the professional should find someone who does.

Of course the amateur will suffer from problems of similar magnitude and he must take the same sort of protective action. Golf itself may be a relaxation in some cases, just make sure it is and not the mental torture which makes many golfers such bad company.

It is not difficult to accept that distractions can have a negative influence on your golf, but not in true in all cases. There are occasions when distraction will work for us.

Emotional problems can develop into very dominating thoughts. They can be difficult to erase but one way to reduce their effect is to talk with someone about them; in other words, find a sympathetic ear. It does help ease the worry but for the sake of your golf do this away from the golf course. If you find this impossible, then arrive at your course a little earlier than usual. Involve yourself with the people you like best, the ones you find it most interesting to be with. Join in with their conversations and discuss with them the topics they dictate. Join them on the practice area or in the clubhouse - wherever - get involved. This way you will be stepping into their mental world and out of yours. Just being inside someone else's "arena" can have therapeutic value. You must all understand the pleasures of being with friends. It does help in these circumstances but be ready to reciprocate when your friends need you. One of the great things about golf is the comradeship of the regular fourball. Just sit back for a minute and think what it means to you.

Going to golf early will not only sharpen up your game if the time is used wisely, it will tone up your complete self.

FEAR

Another very serious interference factor in golf is fear. Fear is a painful emotion caused by impending danger and to the golfer this explains it all. The shot over water, over bunkers, onto tight fairways and of course those short putts. Just a few of golf's situations that can make us tremble and lose control.

A golf course itself has many ways of providing fear; unfortunately there are other ways. Competition alone can cause fear. The expression "put a card in his hand and he falls apart" is a common saying in golf. There is the fear of losing and the fear of winning. Both become more pronounced as a game progresses and if we are not careful, carry on to become the feelings of depression.

The fear of winning is a problem that all golfers have to come to terms with. It is the golfer's main fear particularly at the professional level. It strikes from nowhere at times when we seem to be in full control.

We are hitting the ball well, doing the right sorts of things and all of a sudden it's there. From feeling in control, we are now on the defensive, not just playing safe but playing negatively. We worry about the outcome of the shot because we only see the bad side of things. We provide ourselves with mental pictures which direct our automatic self into playing the wrong shots and become negatively inept in both thought and action. Needless to say, we lose again and all because of the inability to control fear.

The effects of fear are seen every time we play, the main problem being that of shots always coming up short. This can then be compounded by the club face being left open, or closed too soon, and we all know the result. At times, fear will just not allow the club face to come back to square or allow any authority through the ball.

Another effect of fear is the energy loss. We all know that when fear has been part of our day we feel drained of energy and all we can do is go home and "crash out". This even happens to the tour pro and he doesn't even have to carry the bag.

Unfortunately, tiredness does not always wait until we have finished playing. On some days the last few holes can be a nightmare. All of this because the mind is directed by fear and will only consider failure. It does seem strange that when we know exactly what we want to do, we are unable to do it.

We have to accept that the result of being afraid will almost certainly ensure failure. If you stand over the ball and feel that you cannot play the shot, then you cannot expect to play it well. If you only consider hitting the ball out of bounds or if you worry about being short and landing in the water, then how do you expect to hit the ball correctly? If you anticipate failure then you cannot give the shot your undivided attention. You will play the shot too soon or hesitate through to failure. You must take charge of yourself and then play the shot. To do this we need to have a full understanding of relaxation and remember that positive thinking provides positive results. Golfers should concentrate their mind on "what they have to do" and not on "what they do not want to do." Considering what might go wrong is negative thinking.

ANXIETY

Anxiety, the very close associate of fear, forces the golfer to fidget (amongst other things). "Have I forgotten this or that?", "Am I on time?", "The head-up problems". We have all faced them at one time or another and we must identify these restless moods in order to remove them from our thinking.

The anxiety caused through poor preparation can be overcome quite easily and removed with a little forethought. The self doubt we feel on occasions however is a different matter. Very often this doubt is with us from the start of a round or maybe it will appear when we are faced with a difficult shot. To have doubt in our ability to play any type of shot or over club selection, creates uncertainty and negative reactions, and generally results in lost shots.

One very common way of inducing anxiety at golf is to engage in the undesirable behaviour of looking too far ahead. "If I do this" or "we must make par here" bring about unnecessary stress. Do not consider anything that has happened in the past or which may happen in the future unless it is positive. Just accept each shot as it comes along and consider it as a singular challenge. Play one shot at a time. Wishful thinking in golf can let you down, so accept only the completed score card. After all, that's what counts.

As far as distance is concerned or the weighing up of any type of shot, anxiety will be removed to some extent by accepting that our perceptions are not always correct. What the eye sees is not always true and looking at a few optical illusions will support this fact (Chapter 5).

We must know our distances. Distances must be measured and noted on our course plan. Obviously to use this information to its full, we should know exactly how far we hit the ball with each club. I know my distances and how far I take with one stride. I must stress again how important this is in dispelling doubt.

Perhaps it is on the putting surface where golfers feel the most insecure and where the knee trembling is at its worst. The green is a place where it is said "tournaments are won or lost" and how true this is. The demoralising effect of missing those short putts overpowers even the best golfers at times, tightening muscles and scrambling the brain.

Those short putts, particularly on uneven greens, promote so much anxiety and fear and eat up so much nervous energy that it is no wonder we feel exhausted after or indeed before we complete our game. The pressures created by these short putts can creep back into our game, sometimes as far back as the tee shot, so it is important we look a little closer at how we play them.

Firstly we should understand how to relax. A relaxed mind is essential; it will not dwell on negative thought. Secondly we should look at the construction of the green and, just as important, the difference in greens from course to course.

Some greens on most courses are different in pace to the rest but the most noticeable difference is how the greens vary from one course to another. Golfers sometimes find it very difficult to make proper adjustments and this is easy to explain. So much of the feel in putting, as in the golf swing, is performed by our automatic self. Our automatic will always play exactly as it has been trained so if you do have trouble adjusting, remember to use a little more conscious thought and rearrange your "automatic". A change of putter may also help provide the required feel but this is where we enjoy the value of mental rehearsal. If used correctly, it will explain to your automatic the required adjustments. Just play the shot within your mind, then practise the putt, and leave it to your reliable self.

Bumpy greens are one of the golfer's worst problems. They mentally exhaust amateurs and professionals alike; the uncertainty is so unbearable. There are differing ideas on how these greens should be played. If the ball is struck with an upswing, it will have an imparted top spin and run on a better line. This does help but only for the first few inches of the putt. This must logically be a good method however because just like the swing, if it starts off correctly, it has a much better chance of being good.

Anxiety is one of those negative feelings which the golfer can well do without. Its effect can be very easily reduced with a little fore thought and good preparation.

ANGER

Some people seem to generate anger every time they play golf and then think they must punish themselves for "getting it wrong". This they do because they do not understand how to avoid it or just simply because they are dissatisfied with their efforts and feel they could do better. These reasons however really do not matter. Anger is bad for golf and must be removed from the golfer's mind.

Perhaps those golfers who get very angry, do so because of an appreciation of justice and fair play. They do not seem to let any fault go unpunished. In their own eyes, they have made a fool of themselves and their behaviour must be seen to show their disgust in front of others to prove they are doing something about it.

This strange behaviour pattern is unfortunately practised by many golfers. It makes sense to them to punish themselves, often as far as cutting themselves off from their friends or scratching from a forthcoming competition.

There is an old saying "cutting off one's nose to spite one's face". Unfortunately, this not only cuts people off from the people and places they are trying to avoid but also the people and places that could give them a "lift".

Golfers have different ways to vent their anger; some blame others and some blame themselves. Some men blame the ladies and juniors in many different and sometimes disgraceful ways. The ladies blame the men and the juniors sometimes in equally disgraceful ways. The juniors show their dissatisfaction in just the same way as adults do but at some clubs have to play golf under very difficult conditions. Fortunately the young are more resistant to unfounded criticism than adults are but they are being trained through bad example to respond adversely towards others. To many it is always someone else's fault.

Anger at golf should be looked at with a logical mind to find just what it is that makes us behave this way. Immediately we hit a bad shot or find a bad lie or are mentally jostled by some remark, we must be on guard and not, as most of us do, become irate. We must also realise that we cannot keep on absorbing these "punches"; if we do, we become saturated and depressed. We will have hit rock bottom.

Identifying "punches" is not difficult, particularly if you are a sensitive person and realising this we should react to brush it off. We can fend off this aggravation by laughing at it and this is much easier when we are relaxed.

When starting a round of golf we should understand that if we are not in a good mood, then it will be much easier to "go down". Sometimes we start the day partly down and leave little room for the possibility of depressing times in the game ahead. We all know these feelings and should be aware of them. Some days we are just not mentally ready. We should therefore set about finding a way to monitor our moods both before and during play.

GETTING UP IN AN ANGRY MOOD

This may be the result of the previous night's activity but very often there seems to be no explanation. **The cure** is to be aware that this may happen and be ready for it. Be prepared to give yourself a "lift" by remembering the good days. Use your imagination and re-play the good times, maybe an enjoyable holiday, any past or future event to give yourself that "lift". **Smile and be happy.**

STARTING A GAME IN AN ANGRY FRAME OF MIND

This may be produced by past, present or future events. The drive to the course perhaps which can be fraught with danger. There are many fools who drive on the roads and they can "wind you up". A disagreement just before play will have the same effect and if the weather is cold and wet, anger is close at hand. **The cure** is to find time just before play for a few minutes' quiet meditation. Your car will be a good place or even the smallest room in the clubhouse. Tell yourself why you are playing, that you will do your best and that this thinking will give you a definite advantage over the other players. Again re-play in your mind the good days. **Smile and be happy.**

OUR CHANGING MOODS THROUGH PLAY

It is often the case that after starting a game in a good mood, we allow ourselves or others to induce anger. It may be that we are desperate to win and then allow our lack of control or lack of knowledge to shine through. Why should one bad shot or one bad lie ruin all the other good things in golf? **The cure** is to realise golf is not just about hitting golf balls, there are times in between shots which have to be catered for - times which must be devoted to pleasure, even if it is your job. There are many reasons why we sometimes hit bad shots and many of these are outside our control. Bad shots are played by **ALL** golfers. Do not be surprised when it's your turn.

The time when anger usually strikes is when we either think or see we have made a wrong move. We have mishit the shot or played it into the wrong place. Immediately we have done this we must distract ourselves from the ball game and engage in some form of relaxation. We should get into the habit of considering the next shot only when we get to the ball.

Anger is the golfer's worst enemy. It costs more lost shots than any other fault. Get out of the habit of taking a bully round the course with you. Change him for a friend - you know it makes sense.

These different mental problems are bad enough if they are our own but can also have a "rub-off" effect if they belong to someone else. Of all the faults we find in others, perhaps the worst one from our point of view is that of "Old Grumpy". Old Grumpy regards everything as a matter of luck - usually bad. He is always troubled by his ball finding divot holes, lipping out or taking a bad kick. The general problem we find when playing with one of these individuals is that he nearly always drags us down to his level. His conversation centres around his problems and never for one minute is he interested in your game. But then perhaps this grumpy fellow is you?

Golfers who fall into this category should ask themselves - why play golf at all? The "Don't care" attitude that some good golfers seem to show comes from the relaxed and particularly humble way with which they approach the game. Champions look at things realistically, accepting the bad shots and the bad kicks as something that all golfers suffer from. So to all those who have the tendency to lose their cool we say - don't expect perfection - in golf, it does not exist. By far the most important thing is to encourage yourself to enjoy the game because if you study the winners against the losers, who's smiling?

PRESSURE GOLF

There is a golden rule as far as pressure is concerned, and it says that we should take steps to avoid pressure rather than just knowing how to cope with it. To be in control of our thoughts and actions, as we must when we play competitive golf, can only be found with good preparation and an appreciation of our own limitations.

The main things to remember are:

1.   Do not put demands on yourself like, "I must make a birdie here" or "I must make this putt". These demands can only add pressure to what may already be a pressure situation. Birdies will come from good golf.

2. Do not get too "worked up" before a competition. You must stay calm and relaxed before a competition and not eat up the energy required for later. High expectations are demands which all too often result in failure and then depression.
3. Pressure can make you dither about too long with your decision-making particularly when you are over the ball. If you do find that you need time to compose yourself, this should be done before you start your target aiming routine. (Chapter four)
4. Pressure can produce a "jerky" swing, so concentrate on using a smooth action. If you finish your swing in a good position then you should have been good through the ball.

The best way to avoid pressure is to enjoy the day, particularly between shots. Pressure in all cases is self-inflicted and is generally introduced by fear or personal demands. You and only you can overcome these pressures. Smile at golf and it will always smile back at you.

3

POSITIVE GOLF

In golf it is often suggested we should think positively, and without this we are unable to direct ourselves with positive method.

We must try to play our game in such a way as to reduce emotional stress, and remove from our minds the thoughts which bring on feelings of doubt. All golf situations found during play have to be looked upon with good reasoning, and as far as possible, be pre-planned. However, before we can do this we must be sure of just what is positive and what is negative.

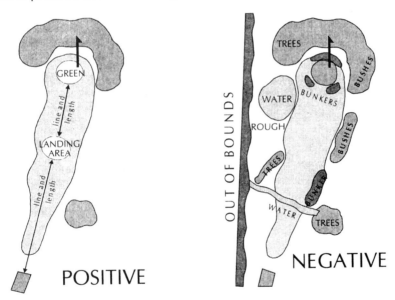

Positive and Negative ways to look at your course plan

If we pose the question "What is positive golf?", we do not always get satisfactory answers. Some believe it to be taking the tiger line or charging the putt and of course this is nonsense. In these two cases it is playing the correct line - predetermined by course strategy - and putting with uninhibited method.

Whilst on the subject of putting, you may remember the time when Johnny Miller seemed to be able to do nothing wrong. In an interview at the time he said that when he was lining up a putt, he could see the line as if it was drawn on the green. This he got through positive thinking and self confidence. It also indicates a good use of imagery.

Our main concern has to be thought which inspires confidence, the feeling of self trust, which comes from knowing we are doing the correct things, playing the correct shots and into the correct positions.

In all shot making, we must first play the shot within our mind. This will provide the trust and understanding needed to play the shot. If, on the other hand, we play the wrong shot within our mind and instil thoughts not conducive to good golf, then all manner of things can happen. If we think out of bounds, into water, into bunkers (we know the feelings; we have felt them so often), we are giving the wrong instructions to our automatic self - the part of our golfing "machine" which can be so reliable. If you will keep thinking about playing into a bunker, then your automatic self will almost certainly follow those instructions.

Positive attitudes are developed by good thinking and good planning. We must educate ourselves to consider only information which is of value to us. Hazards, water, out of bounds - in fact, all of the unwanted visual information presented to us by course layout - must be considered as unnecessary information. All shots must be played to planned landing areas, both on fairways and greens all we need to know is line and length. It is therefore unnecessary to consider anything outside of these areas. We do not need to know that out of bounds exists or that any type of hazard is in the way.

We must use the same method of thinking with regard to other competitors since their mere existence often affects our performance. Our aims have to be to play against ourselves and if we fail to do this, then we give the game away by allowing ourselves too much involvement in things which can only have an adverse effect on our performance.

It is not difficult to follow a method of negative play and believe this to be safe golf. Situations often arise like when we are in a winning position and are afraid of "getting it wrong". This is not good thinking, we are only digging ourselves a hole into which we must inevitably fall. It shows a lack of confidence and a fear of winning which destroys even the "elite" at times. For "safety" we must substitute "sensible". It is sensible to aim for the fat of the green, thus leaving room for slight error of line and - two putts to win - so take them. Many golfers however fail to accept just what the difference is between playing safe and negative play.

To play sensibly, we must accept our limitations: Know what we are capable of doing and never under-estimate or over-estimate our capabilities. Why play short when you know you can get there? Alternatively, if you do not have a club to give a vertical loft and a long carry, then don't go for it. Leave the miracle shot for the desperate to play.

Negative thinking can be brought about by both seeing and thinking and it is not always because of physical hazards. We can bring on the feelings of being overawed by the opposition or by just generally feeling inferior. How often have you gone out to play against someone who has a reputation or a handicap better than your own? Right from the offset you try to play his game, hit the ball as far, score the same gross score, and where does it get you? Nowhere! You can only play within your own capabilities and if you remain this way, then your thinking will be positive.

Being positive is using your common sense to play within the limits of your skills, to be confident in your method and realistic with your thinking. Absolutely nothing else. There is a saying "Think lucky and you will be lucky" and if you consider this saying, you will understand its meaning. It means that positive thinking provides positive method - the confident method which we all seek and which champions have found.

CORRECT LEVEL OF EXCITEMENT

The golfer very often finds that, even if he starts a round in a good mood and his level of excitement is correct, it can alter as the game progresses. This excitement level or "arousal" is an important factor in performance; it indicates the level of interest and involvement a person has in what he is about. It has an optimum level, a level at which we perform at our best. Efficiency falls off if we are above or below this level.

This enthusiasm to play can change if we get too excited and desperate to win. This pushes excitement above the optimum level and boredom will drop it the other way. It can also be reduced by bad weather conditions, which as we all know, can make you wonder why you could not have found something better to do.

Lack of interest can also appear when we get up in the morning. It could be that the previous night's activity is to blame for one's low physical and mental state or just the result of not sleeping too well. Whichever or whatever the cause, picking oneself up can be a difficult process, particularly the older we get. The more often any task in life is repeated, the greater the chances of boredom - one reason why the young golfer often starts favourite. He is more capable of sustaining interest throughout any tournament and certainly throughout one round.

From the professional's point of view, and the committed amateur, living out of a suitcase can leave spare time. How he fills in this time is very relevant to his play. Keeping active away from the course will help towards training a competitive mind but this must be coupled with time for relaxation. Time must be found away from the pressures of both golf and its associated business.

In the past there have been players who, for a short period of time, have hit the high spots. Some are perhaps more famous now for not being able to cope with golf as a game and as a business. The lessons from this should be to slow down, give some of the extra work to someone else and accept that playing the game is what matters - or fame as a player must be short lived.

Alternatively if pure boredom is creating a lack of interest, ask yourself "Why am I bored?" Is it because I am fed up with travelling? Is it because I am sick of the old routine? Or is it because I have forgotten why I play? Just like any other routine we repeat in life, sometimes it is exciting, sometimes interesting and sometimes boring - so it is only natural for any golfer to have his ups and downs. Keeping up an acceptable standard is not so easy.

There are ways around this problem however and lessons to learn. Just as we cannot have instant relaxation or instant concentration, instant interest is not always available. We must constantly remind ourselves why we play and not just between rounds but between shots.

Try putting a note on your course plan after each set of six holes. Let it say "Re-group mentally". Remind yourself why you play and of the need to smile and relax. Whether you give these instructions to yourself or leave it to your adviser does not seem to matter - it has the same effect. The only issue regarding these instructions is their frequency. If weather conditions are not suitable or if you are not feeling up to the mark physically, then the reminders must come more often, as often as each hole.

Interest at the correct level is one of the most important ingredients for consistency. It depends very much on mental fitness but physical fitness plays a much bigger part than many think. Keeping fit both mentally and physically will help maintain what the psychologist calls "optimum performance level".

POSITIVE MOTIVATION

Good golf and enjoyment go hand in hand. To be pleased with yourself is so important when playing golf, because it really does dictate the way we play.

Golf is a game which is governed by the way we feel. We all have experience of this and how quickly our moods can change. For instance a stroke of good luck can raise a smile and bad luck can make some golfers look such fools by the way they react.

Mood and motivation are very much connected. We all know that to have the "bottle" to fight on is a golf requirement, but it must be the right sort of bottle. If a golfer can stay in a good and reasonable frame of mind when things are starting to look a little bleak then his response could be positive. We must stay in control when a competition or match is slipping away, because it is a time to play with determination and commitment **(Figure 7)**. We must remain calm to save making mistakes and making things worse. A smile will help to hit the ball with the quiet authority which produces good shots and not the wild shots developed through aggressive desperation.

Figure 7: Andrew Murray never quits. I thank him for teaching me so much about commitment

The motivation to keep going when things are not going too well can quite easily go the other way and unfortunately become connected to depression. Some golfers do not give themselves the chance to bounce back because their drive to do well is dictated by an aggressive attitude which hits wild shots. They allow themselves to become so depressed that they become uncontrolled in their mind and their efforts. Shots go all over the place and are so often decided by the close your eyes and wish method. These golfers always seem to have the air of having lost a pound and found a penny.

At the 1993 US Masters, Jack Nicklaus was offered positive motivation by his great friend and rival Arnold Palmer. Arnold had started his round with three birdies and Jack set out to chase him. For this he needed to play with controlled determination. He needed to attack the flag with his approach shots and with calm precision. Aggressive hit and hope would just not do, and Jack had a great first round. **(Figure 8)**

On the final day we saw another great master at work, and Bernhard Langer needed the same sort of control. Very soon after his round started, he saw his four stroke lead reduced to one. He therefore followed the same routine as Jack did in his first round and went on the attack with the quiet determination needed to do the job. He understood that to keep in front he had to attack and remain calm.

Figure 8: Jack Nicklaus plays golf with controlled determination

All golfers should look carefully at their own motivation and see if it is controlled or aggressive. Just learn from the masters, when they are in the lead they use their smile and attack. It is no use going on the defensive or playing so called safety golf when in a good position. If Bernhard Langer had gone on the defensive his chances of winning would have been reduced. If he or any golfer who is trying to protect a lead could come to an arrangement with the players behind to also play protection golf, then things would be different. I don't think that he or you would ever be able to make such arrangements.

All pressure situations require a cool head. So when you are in such a situation and need motivation just make sure that it is under control.

EXPLAINING ADRENALIN

Adrenalin is a word often misused by sports commentators and others when referring to the behaviour of sportsmen and women under pressure conditions. How often have we heard the expression "He's got the adrenalin flowing now" to describe the fact that a player is coping with a stressful situation but this is not quite true in the case of the golfer.

To talk in medical terms, adrenalin is a substance your body provides when you are over-excited, in a state of shock, anger or extreme fear. The body secretes it into the bloodstream to create a temporary condition that can greatly increase the body's potential for action.

Remembering that anger and fear are conditions that golfers should guard against, inducing an adrenalin flow that is not controlled is the last thing that a golfer should do. This must not happen, and will not happen, if we remember to "keep calm". The body's adrenalin flow is controlled by another hormone called "noradrenaline" which is extremely important in regulating mood. In "explosive" physical sports like football, tennis and boxing, the flow is created by physical demands, whereas in golf the flow of adrenalin is caused more by mental pressures rather than physical. In golf, if adrenalin does flow, it must be controlled by using our relaxation techniques. Both adrenalin and noradrenaline are governed by the brain and controlled by the nervous system, noradrenaline being essential for controlling stress and arousal levels.

Increased adrenalin flow leads to increased heart rate. If we ever find that we wish to check for stressful effects from hormone secretion, then heart rate is a good measure. A normal heart rate would show a relaxed condition and an increase would show an increase in stress.

As you become more proficient at understanding your own behaviour, you will obviously become more aware of your opponent's behaviour and one thing you will notice is how these hormones affect him. You will notice that when he is angry, his face turns red and when he is afraid, he may go quite pale. These are the tell tale effects of adrenalin.

Limited amounts of stress can be dealt with quite easily. But if we allow ourselves to be under too much stress for too long a period of time, then the adrenalin in our bloodstream will eventually produce a state of exhaustion. We have all at some time or another experienced these effects. Do you remember an occasion when you won a competition? It might have been a trophy or just a round of match play but you felt good, full of life and could very easily have played another eighteen holes right away. You should also remember those feelings that surround losing or not playing a good game. The energy we use to combat the stresses of being beaten either by an opponent or ourselves leaves us very tired and in no way could we play more holes.

Some golfers, after not playing very well, feel that they should go down to the practice ground to "sort out" their game. Yet these are not times for physical practice: they would be much wiser spent on analysing the game that we have just played. Sit in your car or any quiet place and ask yourself what the faults really were. What went wrong? When did it go wrong and why? This is the way we should be spending our time and more often than not, we shall find that the answers we come up with are not physical but psychological.

Emotional reactions in any sport are not always caused by the nasty side of our personality. For instance, being over-confident in any type of competition is unwise. We can very often let a game be lost for this sole reason and we can only blame bad thinking and silly behaviour. There are those times when through winning or playing well, we get very complacent. We become obliging towards the

Notes

other fellow and very soon we are letting him back into the game. Then we realise what is happening and panic strikes. From being in control of the game, we are now on the defensive and all through allowing our determination to drop below that required to maintain complete control. Be more ruthless when in a winning position and do not ease off until the job is complete. If you feel that you should be condescending, leave it until the game is over!

THE POSITIVE WAY TO PRACTISE

If you were to count the number of golfers at your club who spend much or even any time on the practice ground, I would be surprised if you would need a calculator. There will be one or two who always seem to be there and others who only appear when their game is off. **(Figure 9)**

Figure 9: Club practise range. Make sure that you obtain reward for your effort.

Even amongst these, many of them hit ball after ball trying to find out why they are not playing well and more often than not, practising faults until the faults become part of their game. Hitting ball after ball, day after day, will not result in a golf swing jumping out and presenting itself to you. Practise must be in a more logical manner to ensure that we use good method, because whatever we practise we will become good at it.

In the beginning we all had to practise, some carried on with it perhaps because they enjoy the solitude and some because they know how to practise - but most are so much drawn by the challenge of the course or the comradeship of their regular four ball that they never practise. Perhaps to say "never" is a little hard on them - they generally hit two or three balls on the putting green before a competition.

At all professional tournaments they all take time prior to playing for serious practise. Why? you may ask - a professional already knows how to play - but this is not the reason why they are out there. They are there to find how the swing is today. On different days we all have different swings but only slight changes occur and these may be due to the fact that on some days we feel energetic and on others, we don't. It could be the ball in flight will move from left to right, yesterday perhaps it moved the other way. Once we find our swing for the day, we either correct it or use it. Practice before play also loosens the muscles we use for golf.

When you have visited a professional tournament, you must have watched the practice sessions and have noticed the methods used by the pros. Of course there are two different times at which they practise and the methods they use differ accordingly. There is the warm-up play and the work sessions afterwards. After play you will see him or her use their practice routine - play the hook, then the slice, hit some high shots and some low. If it is a windy day, they will hit low wedge shots and short distances with long irons.

At these sessions you will rarely see the pro. alone, particularly the Spanish players. They will be advising each other just as your pro. would advise you at the same type of lesson. So what sort of practice should we do? **(Figure 10)**

Figure 10: Tour event practise range. This exercise is to develop consistency.

Practising all of the different shots we need to be a good player has to be sound advice but for the amateur, there is a principle he should work to. He should practise the things he does well and let a good teaching professional deal with the rest. You may say to this that I am only advertising the professional. Well, to a certain extent I am but what other method is there to stop a golfer practising the parts of his game he finds difficult or can't play? A lesson or two on these problem shots and he could stop you practising faults. Remember, whatever you practise you could become good at it, be it good method or bad.

Another thing to remember about practice is when should we do it and how long a period of time should we stay there?

When we are practising, we will be programming our automatic game, perhaps known as the inner game. It therefore makes sense to work at what we do well and in so doing, boost our ego. This way we are developing the feelings needed to play the perfect shot and building the self trust which removes doubt and is called confidence. All practise sessions must follow a sensible method. We must always spend most of our time playing the shots that we can play well, and when we have played lots of these, then attempt to solve any problems we have in other departments of our game. If you do spend most of your time on problem shots you may practise bad method and avoid the rewards which practise must offer.

We should also understand how long a period of time to hit golf balls before we stop. Many golfers stay until they run out of time, others until their hands become sore and the rest get so frustrated they have to give up. None of these should be the deciding factor.

Notes

You should practise until you start hitting bad shots and then rest. It could be your efficiency drops after twenty balls or fifty balls or any number personal to yourself. This happens to anyone who repeats any type of movement, so stop and take a rest.

It is a proven fact that taking a distracting break as soon as the drop in efficiency starts has an amazing effect when you restart. Your efficiency level will be higher than when you left off. So these calculated breaks must be taken because during the lay-off period, our automatic self is remembering how to play efficiently. If we carry on when efficiency drops, we are again practising faults.

The best way to do this, after you have sorted out your personal number of balls, is to only carry that many to the practice ground. After you have hit them, don't go down and hit them back, go and collect them and at the same time enjoy the day. Look around and see how fortunate you are to be spending this time in such pleasant surroundings. If you are at a driving range, don't buy a large bucket of balls if the last twenty fly all over the place. It is much better to hit a small number and have to break off to buy some more.

Of course some clubs do not have a practice ground so the local driving range will have to do. However the practice of the short game - particularly putting - is catered for at all clubs.

The putting green is perhaps the worst place for practising faults. I see golfers supposedly getting the feel just prior to a competition but even then they either try too hard and get it wrong or they are too casual because it doesn't matter if the ball goes in or not **(Figure 11)**.

Figure 11: The putting green - Do you practise missing?

This again must be changed. All putts must be given the same amount of care. Why practise missing putts? If you start each session with short putts and gradually increase the distance, then you are working to a good pattern. As soon as you start missing too many, either have a rest or move back nearer to the hole.

Have you ever checked how long you normally stand over a putt and how this time period changes when the pressure of competition is on? Why do we change into a person who for some unknown reason has a different thought pattern? All shots should take an equal amount of time to complete. Having said that, competitive pressure will extend the time slightly because pressure will encourage you to take more care.

The set up rituals we have for each shot in golf must be the same however and wherever we play them. The long drawn out enquiry which some golfers make these days will only confuse them and infuriate the people behind.

Maybe the reason for not seeing many golfers using the practice facilities is because they are not satisfied with always getting it wrong. Perhaps if they were to re-think their approach to practice and use profitable methods, then practice would become more enjoyable and of greater benefit.

THE SWING SEQUENCE

Whichever way you swing the club, you may have found that something very strange sometimes happens at this time: what I like to call "ball blindness". During the swing, many golfers completely lose sight of the ball. In fact when taking clinics or playing exhibitions, some top stars will show how to hit with their eyes closed. However, don't be too impressed, it is not difficult.

THE SWING SEQUENCE

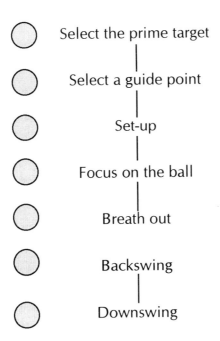

The swing sequence. This series of thoughts are an aid to concentration

Take the full swing sequence. It starts with the search for the prime target. Obviously here the ball is not considered. It does come to mind however on the next link in the chain when looking for the guidepoint and then again when focusing on the target point on the ball. From here we switch our total attention to the swinging of the club, the backswing and then the downswing. This transfer of thought from the set position to the swing overrides the image of the ball and it can completely disappear from view. It may not come into view again until after the completion of the swing when we look up to follow the flight of the ball.

It is not surprising that the ball may be lost in the backswing when we enquire just what the golfer is thinking about in the very small amount of time that it takes to complete the swing. When you ask fellow golfers what they are thinking about during the swing, invariably most are concentrating on the parts of their swing that are causing them problems at that particular time. Along with these thoughts are their basic problems - those of avoiding the hook or the slice. The conclusion is that nearly all golfers go through an extremely confusing routine. Failure to understand how little the mind can cope with during the very small amount of time it takes to complete the golf swing is the cause of many stray shots. Most golfers consider far too much information and although ball blindness may sound strange, in some cases it is inevitable.

Professional golfers, particularly the top professionals, do seem to have a quality that makes them different from most golfers. If the swing to the amateur is a chain of seven links (see diagram), the elite seem to be able to reduce it to six. They change the last two links to one of "what they have to do" and not how they have to do it. The ability to swing the club with little conscious thought of physical movement seems to be reserved for a select few very good golfers. It should be the ultimate aim of us all.

The trained eye of your professional will help him solve most of your physical faults but some faults do not necessarily need his help as they are so obvious. To watch some golfers, one would expect the club to be almost too heavy to swing and the ball itself is apparently glued to the ground. They use far too much effort, half of which would drive a ball 250 yards from the tee. Using too much effort can only create balance problems and this is the cause of many swing faults.

Listening to clubhouse conversation would lead the beginner to believe that the golfer has to be some form of contortionist to get into the positions necessary to swing a golf club correctly. But you only have to look at junior golfers when they swing a club. They look like professionals - but they are young and very supply, you may reply. True the swing, as years progress, might get shorter, the body become less flexible but how many games other than golf seem to have no retiring age? It is not uncommon to read of golfers who are still playing in their nineties so how can it not be a natural movement? At 46 years of age, Jack Nicklaus proved that it is still possible to win the Masters.

The swing itself takes only a very short time to complete - less than a second - and if we extend the set-up time we have an invaluable few moments for extra concentration. Having a simple set thought pattern that leads up to the actual striking of the ball provides a mental set-up as well as the physical one. It helps rid the mind of the fear and confusion that is difficult to dismiss if the shot is entered into too quickly.

In athletics the high jumper and the long jumper both have to use a mental build-up before they start their run-up. Instant action is not reliable enough when we have only one shot and little chance of making up for error. There is a chance, some might say, of making up for a bad shot, particularly if the green is out of reach or if we can chip and single putt on the short holes but the real trouble is that a bad shot can taint the mind.

Keep the swing part of the system simple. One thought to start the backswing - perhaps push the club back along the line - and one thought to start the downswing - pull the hands through to the target. Whatever your personal instructions have to be, use only one of them on each part of the swing. It is not possible to attend to more. If we try, confusion will cause things to go wrong.

Before we attempt to play any shot, we must first play the shot within our own mind. We do this to instruct our automatic self of which shot we wish to play. This is mental rehearsal and it starts with a decision making process.

From your experience, your course plan and "on site" information, decide which shot you have to play. If you do not get this first stage correct, then your confused mind will play a confused and incorrect shot. **(Figure 12)**

Figure 12:
Compose from behind the ball.
Nick Price at
Turnberry

Once you have selected the club and decided how to play the shot, you must rehearse the shot using your practise swing. This again instructs your automatic self with your swing request. You can then enter into your "personal bubble" and follow your swing sequence.

Mental rehearsal is a necessary part of playing all sports - from chess to downhill skiing. If you do not first play your move correctly within your mind, you

Notes

cannot hope to be successful. In golf we have the extra rehearsal of the practise swing, use this correctly and your automatic will fully understand just how you want it to respond.

THE TARGET

Taking our stance is our way of lining up to a target and it is a routine go through. To become consistent we must always set up in the same precise manner as we would in any form of target aiming. To do this correctly we must understand that target aiming has to be at a point - a point on the fairway and a point on the hole. Aim at a tree, a flag, anything that is in line with your chosen line. When putting, aim at any mark on the line of the putt. We simply cannot line up to an area. An easy way to prove this is to play two balls on the putting surface, disregard the holes and putt one ball up to the other. You will be surprised at your accuracy. **(Figure 13)**

Figure 13: Putting one ball up to another is a good practise procedure

Lining up is of particular importance when putting. If we practise sound method and become confident with our lining up, then all that is left is to feel the distance. We should never get into the habit when putting of aiming "just" to the right or "just" to the left of the hole. Decide exactly how far to the right or left and aim at that point. Assuming a line is a waste of time and usually a waste of shots.

After lining up with the target on the fairway or on the green, we should bring the target forward to a guide point and we must decide where the best place for this should be. It should be a few feet in front of the ball position, but not too far in front.

The area of vision within which this target guide point or secondary target should be placed is quite easily decided. Do it on the practice ground, in your office, anywhere when you have a club and a few balls with you. Place the balls about one foot apart in a line on the ground, say seven balls, then stand over the middle ball as if to play a shot and without moving your head, cast your eyes to the left and then to the right to see as many balls as you can. Select a ball either to the left or the right, according to which hand you play. The ball should be within easy reach of your eye movement and this will be the position for your target guide. Having your guide point in view will help you to keep square to the line.

Some golfers do have problems in lining up and for them the best method would be to have the guide point near to the right foot (for the right-hander). This symmetrical set-up will assist them to get square as well as line up. See if it works for you; it is well worth trying. For those who do not have lining up problems then a point in front of the ball will perhaps be of more benefit.

The total procedure should follow like this. Select your prime target, maybe a tree down the fairway, and from standing at the back of the ball in line with that target find a mark on the ground in your guide point position - a discoloured blade of grass, a spike mark, anything that will be in eye range when standing over the ball. Then line up to take the shot. Do this routine before every shot from driver to putter.

One golfer who uses a very obvious line up sequence is Jack Nicklaus. He is very methodical with his set up procedure - one very good reason why Jack was "King Golf" for so many years and can still give the youngsters a good run for their money.

From the start of this routine, one should be processing the mind's eye image of the shot. Very often the golfer, when casting his eye to the target and back to the ball, will be scanning the fairway or even admiring the view. This is an incorrect method. When looking down the fairway the only consideration should be the prime target and here is where we step inside our "personal bubble".

This is how I like to refer to the time at golf when we must isolate ourselves totally from everything and everybody. It is quite a simple thing to do and is something you must learn to do. You cannot swing a golf club with any consistency if you let outside information distract you from the job at hand. I have watched Bernhard Langer do just this. He shuts himself in and his concentration is total. I have also watched him step out with a slight grin showing the satisfaction and pleasure one receives when "getting it right".

These two targets - the one at which we wish to project our ball and the secondary target with which we line up - are joined very closely by a third - the target point on the surface of the ball with which our club must make contact. It is upon this point, or the nearest possible point to it, that our eyes must be focused before starting the swing. Looking at the top of the ball will only encourage topping which as you know is a very embarrassing experience.

Target aiming is the same in all sports, particularly the ones that start from a stationary position. They all demand that we focus on a point.

CONCENTRATION STEPS

There is a definite connection between target aiming and concentration and we should remind ourselves of the routine to use.

The pre-shot ritual should start with a mental rehearsal of the shot we wish to play. This is best done from behind the ball. Check your yardage chart and select your club **(Figure 14)**. Hold the club with "feeling", decide upon the shot, play it within your mind and then make your practise swing.

Figure 14: Woosie and Wobbly. A good course planner is a valuable asset

At this point, move into your "personal bubble" and start the swing sequence of "concentration steps".

The first step is to look at and line up to our prime target (this target we get from our course plan). Move the target to a guide point just in front of the ball and take up the address position. Perhaps another look at the prime target, then the **BACK** of the ball, breathe out and swing the club.

Don't forget that if you have to think about what happens during the swing, make it one thing at the beginning of the backswing and one at the beginning of the downswing. The body movements, after telling yourself to swing, should ideally be left to your automatic self - it is just a matter of feel.

Many of us though have to use some conscious thought; this is the way we have trained ourselves. Theoretically it should be nothing; practically it must be as little as possible.

We must not come out of our bubble until we have completed the shot both mentally and physically. This series of "concentration steps" will provide for you the necessary attention and mental clarity needed to play any golf shot.

RELAXATION

Pressure is something that we all understand. It shows itself at the beginning of a round through the butterflies we experience in our stomach and towards the end when fear forces itself upon us as we consider winning or losing. It has been said that butterflies can interfere with performance but this is not so. In fact they have just the opposite effect. Without this touch of excitement we do not have much chance of being at anything like peak efficiency; however we should understand how to control the feeling and not be left trembling at the knees, as is very often the case.

What happens at times of golfing stress? Mainly this: Too many things turn around in one's mind and cause mental confusion. These thoughts are usually frightening ones - bad shots, bad line, lost ball. Our grip gets far too tight, our knuckles become white, with a tightness travelling along our arms and throughout our whole body. We then grit our teeth but worst of all, we breathe in, hold our breath and then start the swing.

Figure 15: Fuzzy Zoeller - nothing seems to ruffle him

Relaxation is perhaps the main quality of the good golfer so we should teach ourselves how to achieve it. Many champions have the natural ability to relax. Nothing seems to ruffle them. They use very little nervous energy (adrenalin) and this gives them the mental strength to cope with a pressure situation. **(Figure 15)**

We all experience stress in golf, some far more than others and it is essential that we learn how to cope with it. It is not difficult to learn how to do so; all we have to do is understand the basic principles of relaxation and have confidence in the remarkable ability of the human body.

A knowledge of relaxation will help us to reduce stress but better still, it will help prevent it. We shall be able to avoid unnecessary fatigue, caused by the burning up of too much nervous energy and feel far less anxious. The final few holes of an important game will be much easier to play. The secret of relaxation is breathing.

There are obviously many ways of breathing - deep, slow, short, fast, chest, diaphragm - and the one that interests us is breathing from

Notes

the diaphragm. First consider chest breathing. Look at your chest and expand it by taking in a deep breath. This is the type of breathing we do after physical exercise when we are out of breath. Taking in large amounts of air is the way we recover and get back to normal. For relaxation exercises however we use our diaphragm. Look this time at your stomach and expand it by breathing in. Watch it for a while going in and out and you will feel its soothing effect. Allow your breathing to become slower and more shallow, very soon you will feel calmer and more at ease. Whilst out on the course you may feel the need for a deep chest breath: this is a natural reaction particularly after a good shot, a sort of reward for getting things right.

There are three different times at golf when we need to relax: just before the shot, between shots and that very important time, bed time. Remember breathing is always from the diaphragm.

RELAXING OVER THE SHOT

Try this: Stand with a club as if addressing a ball. Have your teeth slightly open, relax your face and feel the relaxation run down to your neck. Shrug your shoulders and then breathe out. This is the point at which you start your swing. You will notice that there is no tightness anywhere and don't worry about breathing in, that will happen naturally. This method should be used for all shots, particularly those three footers.

RELAXING BETWEEN SHOTS

When walking from shot to shot, the rule is to stay loose, hear those flaps on your shoes go slap at every step as you shake your leg muscles loose. I know that some golf shoes do not have lace covers these days, but please use the same action. Shake your arms, hands and fingers as you walk along the fairways just like Miguel Angel Jimenez does. Have you noticed? **(Figure 16)**

Figure 16: Miguel Angel Jimenez is an extremely patient man

Often when playing competitively we are confronted with times of waiting, unfortunately a feature of the modern game. It is far easier at these times to say "perhaps they are playing for the Crown Jewels" than to go off at the deep end, become angry and tighten up. If for some reason the people in front are slow, do not fall into the trap when getting

Figure 17: Arnold Palmer and Tip between shots. One of the most famous partnerships in golf

to your ball of selecting your club, swinging it about and stamping your feet. This is completely the wrong procedure. The situation demands patience **(Figure 17)**. Remember that all shots should follow the same routine so do not start the shot sequence until it is clear to play. The time whilst waiting should be taken up with relaxing movements. Keep calm, patience is a virtue. Was it Walter Hagen who said "Do not forget to smell the flowers"? By this he meant that distracting yourself from playing for a moment will help stop the flow of nervous energy. There is far more to playing golf than just hitting a ball.

RELAXATION BEFORE SLEEP

Some people never seem to get frustrated with their game but unfortunately most of us do. These pressures that confuse the mind can follow us off the course as well as on it. They can make sleeping a problem.

To the amateur, the night before an important game can be a restless one. Professionals, on the other hand, should get used to these situations as much of their golf is competitive and usually lasts more than one day. But if they have had an exceptionally good day then again sleeping could be difficult. If competitive golf does cause lack of sleep, then we must extend our knowledge of relaxation to control it.

Here is one method. Sit comfortably in an armchair with your feet up, or lie down on your back. Perhaps, to start with, the sitting position would be best. In either case, do not cross your legs and have hands by your sides or resting on the arms of the chair.

1.   Watch your stomach and see it going up and down.

2.   Make your breathing out longer than breathing in.

3.   Close your eyes.

4.   Think about your feet, wriggle your toes and relax your feet by making them loose.

5.   Think about your calf muscles and feel the relaxation run past them into your knees and through your thighs.

Notes

6.   Feel the relaxation run up through your body and into your shoulders.

7.   It runs down your arms and into your hands.

8.   Your hands will feel heavy and warm.

9.   Shake your head to relax your neck muscles and relax your face, allowing your tongue to lie on the bottom of your mouth behind your teeth.

10.   You yourself will decide just how long a time you wish to relax. The length of these sessions should be anywhere between two and twenty minutes, according to how much time you have available.

This exercise will leave you in a state of physical "peace", a state of relaxation which makes sleeping easy. Perhaps there will be times in your life, other than through golf, when you will find this technique invaluable.

These are ways of relaxing the body but through your own experience you should understand that to relax the mind you must think only about things that please you. Remember the good games, particularly the good shots, and sleep will follow.

RELAXING THE MIND

Controlling the mind and moods is achieved quite easily by dictating the image on your mind. Distracting thoughts, particularly the ones that cause you to worry, are much easier to control when the body is at ease. Relaxing the mind therefore is a simple extension of relaxing the body.

We all know what types of images we like and with training we should not find it too difficult to keep them in mind by constantly being aware that unpleasant thoughts can creep in and produce depressing or distracting pictures. The images we should look for when trying to sleep should perhaps be the first hole of your favourite golf course. Picture yourself standing on the first tee, look at the view, search out the view in detail, examine the main features - that well positioned tree - and be sure exactly where your drive will finish (in that perfect position). Pleasing thoughts.

Use this image every time you wish to rest or sleep and it will be your personal thought towards conditioning your sleep pattern. Eventually through associating this image with sleep you will find that it will automatically lead to reduced tension and peace of mind.

Changes tend to happen quite frequently in thought pattern; the mind could be likened to a bird in a tree, always on the move from branch to branch. When change does happen, be aware of it and gently ease back that pleasing picture into your mind. In time you will become much quicker at identifying these changes and the removal of negative thoughts will become easier.

Figure 18: An interesting shot. Paul Way recovering from a wayward drive

Out on the course we obviously use a different approach because peace of mind on a golf course is achieved by positive thought. Refuse to let yourself think of any hazard or difficulty, in fact anything at all that is negative **(Figure 18)**. Replace the word difficult in your golf dictionary with the word interesting so that some shots are more interesting than others. Be conscious of the confusing effects of fear and anxiety; it may help to know that over half of the nerves that feed nervous activity back to the brain are in the hands and face. Remember to smell the flowers.

THE INNER GAME

The body movements made by the golfer are directed and guided in one of two ways. One set of instructions are provided by the way we think, both before and during the swing. The other way is through what is best called our automatic self. Every golfer has these two selves - one conscious, the other subconscious - and the "elite" of golf have control over them both. Others have limited control and the poor old duffer is in real trouble.

Our automatic self is the part of us which controls many body functions, breathing for instance. We do not have to think about doing it - it happens on its own, even when we are asleep. We do not have to look at our feet when going up or down stairs, our other self deals with it.

In all sports, and particularly in golf, only a small part of the movement patterns involved at any one time is under the direct guidance of the conscious mind. The remainder is controlled or guided below the level of conscious awareness by the automatic mind.

Notes

It is of the utmost importance therefore that we look upon practice as a method of training or programming the automatic mind with positive and correct procedures. This way we will ensure that we can produce actions which are consistent and reliable.

Unfortunately the power of the automatic mind can be positive or negative and it is at times of stress that we find whether or not we have been using the correct training methods. The automatic mind will be consistent and reliable whichever way we have trained it.

This other self can be programmed in two different ways and one way is on the practice ground. If we adhere strictly to the methods explained by a good teaching professional our game will become reliable. The other way is practise within your own mind whilst you are in a state of deep relaxation. This is something you can do as often as you like, particularly if you cannot find time or the facility for physical practice.

Figure 19: Seve in full flow. His swing is majestic

To do this, you should decide beforehand just which mental pictures you wish to use. If, for instance, you have been troubled with your tempo, then perhaps you should decide to watch Seve Ballesteros **(Figure 19)**. Close your eyes and watch Seve swing the club with his elegant flowing style. The rhythm could almost be set to music. After a while place yourself into his position and before long you will be able to feel yourself copying his swing. You can, during these sessions, smell the grass if you try.

When you are out on the course, imagery can be used in similar ways. You can use the talent of someone else to produce confidence in your own shots. If you happen to be a beginner or just dissatisfied with your own game, imagine you are someone else who does play the shot well. He may be your hero or one of your regular playing partners. See him doing it and then place yourself into his position. This way you will be automatically using the talent of someone else to your own advantage and find confidence in shot making.

As you may be aware, the mental game demands we have control over our emotions. Things like anger, fear and anxiety are parts of our game we can do without. These faults can also be corrected during sessions of deep relaxation. We can replay the good days to help recall the feelings associated with "getting it right". It will show us the way to overcome those feelings of hate and dislike for ourselves, which accompany poor play.

These methods should be practised as often as you possible can. You will then be training a good automatic game and also helping the mental rehearsal technique which is so invaluable prior to shot making. These lessons will make your automatic game positively reliable and develop self confidence.

Although this method of inner game training is a very powerful system, some sportsmen and women do find it quite difficult to master. There is fortunately the other method to train or correct your automatic game. Since golf began, the champions have used it. They hit ball after ball with good method, building an automatic game to rely on. Which ever way you choose to practise, make sure that you use your time wisely.

PROGRAMMING YOUR AUTOMATIC

One good time for programming is prior to a competition. Before every game, and preferably the night before, you should visualise an ideal round on the course you have to play. This will tune your swing and reinforce your willingness to follow the course plan. Alternatively you may decide to improve your mental attitude. We can all lose our cool on occasions and mentally repeating our swing sequence whilst relaxed will harden our resolve to remain in the placid mood needed for golf.

A typical relaxation session for programming your automatic game should go like this.

Decide before you relax which part of your game needs attention. It may be you need to look at your putting or your short game. Your driving may need smoothing out or maybe you may wish to analyze the last game to replay the good shots and examine the others.

So decide on the type of programming you wish to follow and list in your mind the shots you will mentally rehearse. Writing these down on paper will help you remember them. I often play my last round which is clear in my memory and perhaps this is the approach we should take.

We are now ready to relax and it would also help if you have memorised the relaxation steps (as I explained earlier). Sit in an easy chair in the most peaceful place you can find. Place your feet side by side, your arms on the chair arms, your fingers just hanging over the ends. Watch your stomach going up and down as you breathe using your diaphragm. Gradually slow down your rate of breathing by making breathing out longer than breathing in. Once you feel the soothing effects of this type of breathing, close your eyes. Make the relaxation "journey" from your toes to your face, finishing by placing your tongue on the bottom of your mouth and behind your teeth.

Remain in this state of peace for another two or three minutes, then take yourself into your imaginary world and back onto the first tee of the last game you played. You will see quite clearly the same surroundings and the same situations, the only difference being you can now dictate the type of shot you play. If you were dissatisfied with the shot you played last time then change it for a good one.

You may at first, when playing these imaginary games, only be able to "see" yourself playing the shot. But after a while you will develop the ability to "relive" the shot, to feel the smoothness of the swing and see the results of your efforts. Play all the shots you planned and repeat them if you have time but most of all, remember how satisfying these shots are to play. Remember the joy and pleasure of playing the perfect shot and you will be programming yourself with feelings which you will be able to recall. If ever you do play a bad shot, then play it again just as you would like it to be played.

Some people find these sessions easy to play, others take a little time to get the feel of it. Persevere, everyone can do it.

If you are to believe in the usefulness of this method of learning, you only have to try it. It seems that the only rule you have to follow is to get on with it. Just persevere with the "exercises" and improvements will happen, even if you don't believe in it at all.

I once asked a very talented young club professional to play the first hole at Wollaton Park Golf Club, Nottingham. A delightfully scenic course and one you should play if you are ever in the area. We were in my study at the time discussing his mental game so it had to be played within his own mind. He told me afterwards that he played the shot twice. The first shot he disliked, the second finished in the ideal position, left of centre and long, exactly where he wanted it to be.

After the game the following day I asked him where his tee shot actually finished. His reply was "Exactly where it finished last night. The pictures were exactly the same, it was just like an action replay".

Another young professional once asked me if I could help with his chipping and pitching. The rest of his game was OK but if he missed a green he could almost guarantee to muff the next shot. His confidence had gone. Why?

Again we were in my study and when he was fully relaxed, I asked him to take his wedge and a bag of balls onto the practice area at his club and play a few shots. After a while I asked him how it went.

"The problem is" he said "I am alright until I am on the downswing and just about to hit the ball, then the club will not go through". So we sat and discussed why. The conclusion we came to, and it cured the problem, was that he could not decide on the type of shot he had to play. There are many ways to play these shots and if you don't pick one, how can you mentally rehearse the shot. His problem was being indecisive, which produced such indifferent results.

This method of learning is not just advantageous to golf. It can be used to better performance in any type of sport from tennis to shooting. In skiing, the downhillers could not manage without it. It benefits public speaking and helps in any of life's situations where special techniques have to be learnt.

When your body is relaxed it opens the door to your automatic mind. You can see things more clearly, think more clearly and use to good advantage an experience you may have previously thought was just "day dreaming".

IMAGERY

Imagery or mental rehearsal is used by all top sportsmen to ensure peak performance. Let me explain what it is. There are two things to remember; what to image and when to use it. But first, what is imagery in golf?

Everyone has a wonderful imagination. You can imagine yourself doing anything at all, both good and bad. In golf we try to dictate these images we see in our mind to be positive and good. We see ourselves playing good shots, particularly at the mental rehearsal stage prior to playing a shot. We can imagine anything we like.

Have you ever imagined you were someone else and tried to play a golf shot the way he or she does? Children do it in all manner of ways. It is a very good proven way to success - I do it myself. When I have an "interesting" bunker shot to play, I imagine how Gary Player would play the shot, become Gary Player for a few moments and play the shot as if I were him. **(Figure 20)**

There is another way to use imagery and improve your game. If previous experience suggests you need to play a particular type of shot on a certain hole, play it on the practice area before play. This is another reason for the pre-game knock-up. Play the shot as

Figure 20: Gary Player has perfected the bunker shot

Notes

often as you like, then when the time comes to play it "for real", use your imaginary skills to take yourself back to the practice area. Play the shot you already know, recalling all the confidence and the satisfaction of playing a successful shot.

IMAGING AND OPTICAL ILLUSIONS

Imaging the shot is a very big part of the professional game. As I have already stated, line and length are positive but a positive image, both of the landing area and the shot, is vital.

It may not at first seem obvious that we should be concerned with a positive image until we accept that our perceptions are not always correct. This point can be emphasised by looking at a few optical illusions.

I am sure that at some time or other, you have completely misread the distance of a golf shot. There must have been times when you have not just misjudged by one club but by perhaps two or even three.

Sometimes landing areas can appear to be large, particularly if one can see the whole area of them. A fairway landing area on an up-slope can look closer than it actually is. Alternatively if the fairway is flat, with water or any type of hazard to hide the landing area, then it can promote a different and distorted image.

It is important to know landing areas so as to enable us to make a correct mental picture. This will help promote a more positive and confident feeling when taking the shot. Imaging is the main reason for walking forward to examine the landing area; it helps enhance the mental scene.

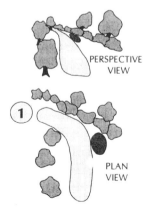

Figure 21:
Perspective Illusion

When standing on the tee or at an approach shot, it can be off-putting if the target area appears to be small. The tunnelling effect of perspective will make a target area appear to be small when in reality it is very large. **(Figure 21)**

There are three different conditions that present themselves to us when looking at our target. One is a full view, another a part view and third no view at all. Surprisingly, having no view at all of the target area does not seem to promote quite as much fear as does the small view. This is because one only has the "mind's eye" to produce the mental picture. If on the other hand the mental picture is influenced by the visual picture, then distortion may take place. Being unsure of the mental picture is the condition that causes the indecision in club selection. We have all had problems with our club selection and know that if doubt does enter our mind, then unsatisfactory shots usually follow.

It is obvious therefore that we should study landing areas very carefully and that when planning a course, we must find time to stand in them specifically to store in our memory the picture of their layout. Standing in them will imprint the picture by searching out their most prominent features. This way you will remember them and be able to recall that mind's eye view when you need it.

In all cases when pressure shots induce nervousness of any degree, physiological changes can take place in any golfer. Pulse rates can increase to produce over-active muscles and this we can do without. So our preparation and planning of a course is as much to improve our mental and visual game as our practical game.

OPTICAL ILLUSIONS

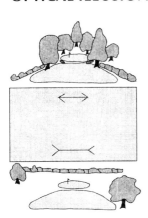

Figure 22: The Muller-Lyer Illusion

The Muller-Lyer illusion **(Figure 22)** is a very strong one and needs very little explanation. Both lines are the same length but the one that has the arrowheads pointing outwards seems to enclose the line and make it appear smaller than the other example. We can take this illusion and place it in a golf course situation and see just how it interferes with our judgement of size. You may also be interested in the other examples illustrated. One shows perspective interference and looking at the other you will see dark areas at the corners of the squares which are not actually there. **(Figure 23)**

Another interesting illusion is that provided by shadows. One of golf's major problems occurs when one has to play directly into the rising or setting sun. It leads to that inevitable head up when looking for the outcome of the shot before the swing is complete. Fades become slices and draws become hooks, emphasising again the need for a clear mental image.

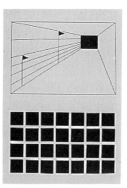

Figure 23: Perspective Interference and Black and White Squares

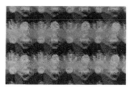

Figure 24: The Egg Box Illusion

As we are all aware, lighting is usually from above, either from the sun or some artificial light source.   If on occasions however the illumination arrives from another angle, then optical illusions may occur. The glare from water may light up a rolling fairway against a dark background and alter the contours of the fairway. The sun's rays may throw tree shadows across a flat fairway, giving a striped effect and making the fairway appear to have humps and hollows. If a source of light does change position (as does the sun at different times of the day) a reversal of depth can take place. It is known as the pseudoscope effect. The illustration **(Figure 24)** will explain this. After looking at the picture, turn the book upside down and look at the picture again. You will see that the humps change to hollows.

So remember, not everything we see with the naked eye is correct; mistakes can be made both of distance and size. Illusions are generated within our own minds and understanding this should emphasise the need for good planning.

Planning the way to play your course perhaps needs an example although some points are obvious. It would be silly to play a competitive round on a course that demands blind shots without first having a practice round to sort out the line and length. The speed of the greens could vary from what you are used to, so playing a different course has its obvious reasons for planning.

PLANNING TO PLAY YOUR OWN COURSE

The first hole on my course is a short par 4 - on an average summer's day, a drive and a wedge. It dog legs from right to left with a drainage dyke running the full length of the hole along the right edge of the fairway, the semi-rough being non-existent. Over the dyke are large trees growing quite close to each other providing a wall of foliage. The left side of the fairway, the inner side of the dog leg, is an area of bushes and small trees. The tallest trees are nearest the fairway and 160 yards from the medal tee. A good drive therefore could cut off the dog leg; but if you do decide to take this line, the fairway in your landing area (even if you do hit a good drive) is rather uneven and could give a difficult lie.

The green is on two levels and as usual the lower part is at the front and is quite soft (the water drains that way). This can cause a problem when the flag is on the back third of the green. On any green, slopes between tiers must be taken into account when planning the putt. They should be avoided if possible. Most slopes that join two levels have to be mowed from top to bottom so that putting up or down the slope is affected by grain. Pace can be noticeably different.

All this sort of information should be taken into account when planning your lines. The landing area is obvious; it has to be just past the knee of the dog leg requiring a straight drive down the left of centre of the fairway. Distance is not as important on this hole as it would be on a long par 4 but the approach shot has to be planned to suit the flag position. If the flag is on the back tier, then a low shot will take the ball up onto this hard section. A high stopping shot is required when the flag is forward.

Once you have decided upon your lines and landing areas, you should put the reasons for your decisions out of your mind. They could become irrelevant and off-putting distractions.

You may have noticed that there has been no mention of bunkers. They are there but did not need to be considered. Think of them only if you need to play short of them when planning landing areas.

There may be holes on your course where you could consider two plans determined by your drive. Take, for instance, a hole for which two plans are possible. If you drive into a position that we call "A", a certain hazard is then out of play, that is, the hazard is easily cleared with the next shot. On the other hand, if you drive into position "B" then the hazard is still left in play and you must play your next shot short of it.

If two plans are possible, do not allow yourself to play the second shot from plan "A" if your drive is in position "B". Do not try for miracle shots. This is a stupid way of trying to make up for a bad drive. The chances of these shots coming off are quite remote and should never be used unless there is no other option. We must accept that "hit and hope" shots are not reliable. Make your plan and stick to it.

Notes

NEW COURSE REQUIREMENTS

The information we need to play courses with which we are not so familiar, needs to be sorted out before we can attempt to play the course seriously. With good planning we can play a course with confidence and without the fear and apprehension of the unknown which so often leads to poor scoring.

When playing a new course we may find difficulty in selecting the correct club or feeling the pace of the greens, but this missing information we can find if we set about to "read" the course. There is an ideal route around all courses and we have to decide upon the chess type moves needed to play with the calm confidence required for good golf.

You may feel at first that a suitable yardage chart will remove most of the doubt and uncertainty and to a some extent it will. But what the yardage chart does not offer is the positions of the "fairway greens" which you may like to call your landing areas.

It is not positive golf to stand on the tee, hit the ball into space and expect it to arrive in a suitable place from where to play the next shot. We must know exactly where we want the ball to finish, because only then can we have faith in our club selection and be able to line up correctly to a predetermined target.

Finding these landing areas is one reason for a practise round. Take plenty of time and get it right. It will not be in the same place for everybody because we all hit the ball different distances and of course it depends on how you "shape" the flight of the ball.

Another reason is to find the layout of each green. We need to know if the greens are level, if they have more than one tier, and their dimensions. If there is a slope we need to know which way it slopes. For instance if a particular green slopes from front to back we may have to pitch onto the front of the green to avoid going over the back. If there is a slope from back to front then we can be more bold with our club selection.

Setting out course strategy is an exercise in common sense. There is not too much information to gather but is important information. We must understand the best way to solve the problems placed before us by golf course architects then we can set about beating the course which should ensure that we beat the opposition.

GOLF CLUB TECHNOLOGY

The search for a better understanding of our golf must include all aspects of the game. There is the mental side, the physical side and the equipment we use to play the game. All this knowledge and effort is needed to enable the golfer to find those all important feelings of confidence which are so important at all levels of the game.

The golf club itself is an engineering structure. A structure which has to supply a force to a golf ball, be able to withstand that force and then return to normal. It has to bend and twist for many reasons and be of a enough weight to propel the ball over large distances. It must also be of a weight that can be under the control of the golfer when he or she swings it.

The standard golf club has to fit a large range of different golfers. Some are tall, some are short, some are talented and some are not so talented. There is a wide range of different features and abilities in the people who play the game, and golf clubs have to be quite user friendly to cover the spread.

The golf club is quite a sophisticated piece of equipment and if it is to suit your game then you should understand how it works. To do this we must take a look at the technology contained within it and make sure that we take full advantage of modern technology.

We have perhaps thought that a golf club is just a lump of material fitted on the end of a stick. Well that's exactly what it is, but the shapes and weights of the heads, shafts and grips are extremely important.

Figure 25: Fred Couples is a favourite to watch wherever he plays

In recent years, and this perhaps started with toe and heel weighted clubs, scientists have been having more say in design and development. The old design philosophy of "If it looks good then it has to be correct," is hopefully gone forever. Clubs are now becoming more user friendly and not before time. Even though we are now seeing club designs which Fred Couples once referred to as ugly. **(Figure 25)**

There are some very important features in golf club design and they show that this lump of material on the end of a stick with a "rubberish" handle is a very scientific piece of equipment indeed.

Golf club design is centred around two features. One is to help the golfer hit the ball over varying distances and the other is in producing ball spin. These two features are inseparable but there are times when they vary in relation to each other.

Figure 26: Club and ball impact

The ball starts from rest and in half of one thousandth of a second (club and ball contact time) it can be spinning at up to about ten thousand revolutions per minute. I say "about" because it is very difficult to measure spin and the rate is more of a calculation than a measure. Incidentally, the contact time between club and ball is surprisingly the same whatever the shot. **(Figure 26)**

This spin decides the flight path of the ball and we all know that if the spin axis is not somewhere near horizontal, then it will either slice or hook. Spin not only flights the ball left or right, it also has a big influence on distance. If a ball contains high spin rates it will fly high and in an ever increasing path until it falls almost vertically back to earth. This is the type of shot and trajectory we need to approach the green. However, if we are looking for distance, we need a much lower and less climbing trajectory so that the ball lands with more forward momentum. This will allow the ball to run after it hits the ground and for this shot we need less spin.

There are a number of ways by which the club imparts the spin. They are loft, head balance, shaft, shaft balance, grooves, club head speed, and added together they become a very powerful mechanism. The part played by the golfer comes mainly through club head speed. There is some effort from the golfer with regard to force and we all know that the force between ball and club face is very large. In fact, it is in the order of one ton, but club head speed is the major component. Players like Greg Norman and Nick Faldo get most of

Figure 27: Greg Norman generates enormous club head speed

their spin through being able to generate fast club head speed. They achieve most of this by having a very large swing arc. **(Figure 27)**

Many golfers are of the misunderstanding that if we put more weight in the head of the club we will then hit the ball further. This can be corrected by looking at the work of a scientist called Daish. In his book called the Physics of Ball Games, he shows that the weight of the club head will determine how fast we can swing the club. This seems quite obvious when we think about it, and his graph shows that clubs with head weights between 150 and 300 grammes all hit the ball about the same distance, if the shaft length remains the same. This is because we swing them at different speeds. The heavier the club the slower we swing it.

The major change in spin throughout the range of our clubs is determined by the loft in the club head. As you know this loft varies from as small as seven degrees on a driver to as much as sixty degrees on some of the modern pitching wedges. The larger the loft the higher the spin. That may seem as far as it goes with respect to loft until we discover that there is such a thing as dynamic loft.

When we swing a golf club the shaft bends. These bends are a significant factor in both spin and distance and the phase of the swing from the top of the backswing through to impact is very interesting. **(Figure 28)**

At the top of the back swing we stop the club and reverse its travel. We do this with our hands arms and shoulders, but the club head still wants to carry on the same path and so the shaft has to bend. During the beginning of the downswing this bent shape returns to straight, carries on to bend the opposite way, as does the pendulum of a clock, and then straightens out again. This happens in the first phase of the downswing. We are now at a position where the wrists start to uncock forcing another bend in the shaft. It then repeats the straight and forward bending procedure prior to the impact position. As you can see from the photographs the shaft at impact is bent in a fashion which gives the club head a dynamic loft. So the loft at impact is decided by both the static manufactured loft and the flex of the shaft.

Figure 28: Shaft just after impact

To some extent the dynamic loft has been understood for some years. Many golfers particularly professionals know that if they add lead tape to a golf club head, it makes the ball fly higher. This is because the added weight put more bend in the shaft. Some golfers find this an advantage but they should be careful, extra head weight will increase the swing weight and make the club more difficult to swing. The swing weight can be "fiddled" back to its original number by increasing the length of the shaft but again do be careful, this will only make the club even more difficult to swing. Yes you may hit a good one now and again with this arrangement, but they won't always be as straight as you would like them to be.

"Swing weight" is the measure used by manufacturers to ensure that there is consistency in manufacture. Clubs are balanced about a point 14 inches from the grip end of the club. **(Figure 29)** For this particular swing weight machine, a weight is slid across the beam until the whole arrangement balances about a pivot protruding from the bottom of the beam. Along the length of the beam over which the weight slides is a scale and this ranges from A to F. In between each letter the distance is divided into 10, each small division is equal to one "swing weight" and most manufacturers use the numbers between C7 and D3. If you cannot follow my explanation please ask your professional to demonstrate to you, I am sure that he/she will be only too pleased to do so.

Loft and force decide the launch angle of the ball. We all know this from our experience of hitting golf balls. When we play full shots with a wedge, and particularly if we use a ball with a soft cover and the greens are receptive, the ball stops dead or spins back towards the player. When we play pitch shots we get less dynamic loft and slower speeds. We therefore produce less spin and the ball rolls on. The influence of the force changes the launch angle. Short shots have a higher launch angle than full shots. So the height achieved by the full shot is provided by the increased spin.

The bending and twisting of the shaft are even more involved in the spin mechanism. You can accept my explanation of this or you can prove it to yourself by making a simple model club which has no loft.

Figure 30: Spin device demonstration

This is not difficult to make and it will be a worthwhile exercise. Use a block of wood or metal about the same weight as a driver head (205 grms) **(Figure 30)** with an old shaft glued into a centre position. The idea is to use this club to hit a golf ball about 12 inches into the air and then catch it.

First try to hit the ball out of the what would be the toe of your club i.e. on the right side of the shaft. Then use the left side of the shaft. You will see that the ball spins in opposite directions. The spin is generated by the club twisting about the centre line of the shaft whilst the ball is in contact with the club and this is known in the trade as gear effect. When we play the game, a ball hit out of the toe produces a draw shot and out of the heel a fade shot, providing that the face is square to the line of flight. This happens because of the rocking motion of the head and is not just characteristic of shots which impact the left and right of centre.

You will see this in the next part of your spin experiment. Hit the ball at a position in the bottom of the head and then the top, both hits should be in line with the shaft. You will see that the ball hit at the bottom will give back spin and the one out of the top an over spin.

If it were possible to hang your model head in space, you would see that the lines would cross the middle of the head. With a shaft attached, the horizontal line moves nearer to the hands as shown in the diagram. Gear effect is real, and even in the very small period of time when the ball is on the club face, very large spin rates can be generated.

Spin device with spin lines

It should now be a little more easy to appreciate the spin mechanism. However club head designers do have problems positioning these lines about which the club head twists, because golf club heads are not a regular shape and the shaft does not enter the centre of the head.

On the old fashioned iron "blade" clubs, the lines are not very beneficial to the average golfer. The twisting line, as we might call it, which goes through the centre of the "sweet spot" is quite close to the hosel and the spin line is a long way from being horizontal.

Things start to become more acceptable in the quality cavity back club and hollow metal woods. Weight is transferred by the club designer to parts of the head which moves these lines into a more profitable place. To do this, head shapes have to change and what Fred Couples said is absolutely true. Head shapes are becoming ugly and perhaps they will become more ugly if the manufactures do not come to some compromise with the "eye appeal golfer."

There is yet another element in the spin mechanism and this involves the flex and twist of the shaft. A shaft which offers more twist action will create more spin because of the greater gear effect. Therefore a shaft which has more resistance to twist will offer less sideways spin and therefore less fade and draw. A shaft which is stiff in flex, particularly in the tip section, will also offer less spin in the vertical plane, again because the gear effect is less, and the ball will run further when in it contacts the fairway. Obviously, golfers who need help to get the ball into the air will benefit from the extra dynamic loft provided by a more flexible shaft.

So from this we know that a stiff shaft will produce less spin and therefore greater distance. If you do have difficulty getting the ball "up" then you can take advantage of dynamic loft through using a more flexible shaft. Many golfers would actually gain more benefit by using a stiff shaft and a club head with more loft.

You should tee up high for the driver since a ball hit high in the club face will produce less spin and more run when the ball makes contact with the fairway. You should tee up low if you are looking for the best possible backspin to put stop on the ball. When you have to play a ball which is sitting-up in the semi rough, it will almost certainly have a high impact position on the face and this explains what is known in golf as a "flyer".

Grooves are the most talked about part of the spin mechanism. This is because we have always been told that grooves stop the ball sliding up the club face. If there is any slip then we lose some of the spin. Scientist Bill Gobush says that for the majority of time when the ball is in contact with the club, the ball "sticks" to the face. He says that there is a small amount of slip at the beginning of the contact time and again just before the ball parts company with the club.

The one thing left to discuss in the spin generation mechanism is the input from the player. All things considered, the important factor is where on the club face do you impact the ball. You know that to hit the ball with the same force and flight, you must impact the ball on exactly the same face position for each shot. If you hit a ball away from the sweet spot (torsion line) then some of the force which is supplied will be lost in opening or closing the club face. If the club face does open or close during the time when the ball is on the club face then the ball will not fly straight. This is just as important with a putter as with any other club in the bag. From my putter tests made under laboratory conditions, a ball hit out of the toe or heel by my putting machine, will only travel 3/4 of the distance a perfect hit.

You must now do the final test. Mark your practise balls with a felt tip pen and face the mark so that when you hit the ball the felt tip mark will transfer to your club face. You will find that even when playing from a flat and even lie that there will be quite a spread in the mark positions.

Perhaps now you can reconsider your practice schedule. It is unreasonable to believe that you can find a physical method which will ensure the balance and timing needed to hit the ball out of the same spot on the club face for every strike. You will regularly hit the ball left, right, and centre. Sometimes you will play the ball short and sometimes long. These variations in line and length can be very frustrating and interfere with your mental game. You have to be able to deal with them.

Which Golf Ball?

The golf ball is another very complicated engineering structure. It has so many varying characteristics and manufacturers change dimple patterns, materials and overall construction to suit many conditions. This makes it very difficult to identify which ball to use.

The ball is discussed by many golfers as being a determining factor in achieving distance, but does it really matter? Of course it does, we are told this by the golf ball manufactures and they spend large amounts of money in research and advertising to state this fact.

Having said that, I recently read that golf is not just a long driving competition. Well, it doesn't always seem that way to me and I say that after having played the game for more than 30 years. It's a bit like saying that golf is only a game and it's the taking part which matters. No it's not, as I've said before, we play to win and we must take every advantage we can to achieve that aim. Hitting the drive out of sight is the ambition of most golfers. The players at all golf clubs who hit the ball a long way are admired by those who can't.

Golf balls used today are of three different types and each are of different construction. There is a one piece ball which is used on driving ranges and this does not travel as far as the balls we use to play the game. They are made this way for obvious reasons and I don't like hitting them because they offer such a course feel.

The three piece ball has been around for a very long time. It consists of a core which can be hard or soft and around this is wound a continuous rubber thread which is then rapped in a dimpled cover.

The two piece ball which is supposed to be a new invention, (the feathery was a two piece ball) has transformed the game somewhat in recent years. Not just because there are more variations in their play-ability, but they last longer and are better value for money. A poor hit on the old balata ball can render it useless.

When considering which ball is best for you, perhaps we should first look at what some of the "academic" men of golf have to say.

In his book GOLF THE SCIENTIFIC WAY, Alastair Cochran of the R&A edited a collection of chapters from various authors regarding all areas of golf. In the section on golf balls, Michael J Sullivan and Terry Melvin (Spalding Sports, USA) talk about spin. They state that

Notes

cover hardness is directly related to spin. Ball compression also has some influence on spin, but the bottom line from their tests show that a three piece ball with a hard centre and a soft cover will generate the fastest spin.

Mikio Yamada (Dunlop Japan) looks at the effects of temperature on the ball. He shows that a reduction in the temperature of a golf ball reduces the distance travelled more in three piece balls than in two piece balls. Alastair Cochran goes on to say that on cold days when the temperature is down to zero, a wound balata covered ball would travel 10 yards less than it would if the temperature were 23 degrees centigrade. He also says that on a cold day the air is denser and that this would cut a further 5 to 7 yards off the carry of the ball.

The very distinguished golf ball scientist Bill Gobush (Titleist USA) says in his paper on "Spin and the Inner Workings of the Golf Ball", that the emerging picture of modern day ball research is a quite complicated one. He could not be more correct and it makes it very difficult for the club golfer do decide which ball to play.

So perhaps the paper presented at the Second World Scientific Conference on Golf 1994, called "Does it Matter What Ball You Play" by T. Hale, P. Bunyan and I Sewell, will give a simple answer. It suggests that for golfers up to 18 handicap, more distance would be achieved if they used a two piece surlyn covered ball. Above this handicap, golfers should use a three piece surlyn covered ball. It also goes on to say that from "casual observation" golfers have to choose between trying to hit the ball a long way and trying to reduce their handicap. If handicap reduction is important to them, they should invest in the more expensive soft covered ball and spend more time practising their short game.

If you now remember what the input of a golf club makes to spin rates, then the ball for you is a relationship between your clubs and any particular ball. So what suits one golfer does not necessarily suit another. From my own experience I know which ball travels the furthest for me with the clubs I use and I am sure that you know which one suits you. I also know which ball to play with when the greens are hard. If you can not make up your mind, you should make every effort to do so. Choosing a golf ball is not easy, but you should experiment and find the best one for your game, because knowing that you have the best ball gives you the added confidence to hit the ball with some authority.

It is important to have confidence in your equipment and it would make sense to follow the advice of Hale, Bunyan and Sewell. If you

Notes

Figure 31: Seve playing from the rough. His ability to play the recovery shot is something to admire

want to win, and this is really why we play, then being competent with recovery shots will do wonders for your confidence. If you are confident on and around the greens, then you will be more positive with your approach shots. This in turn will make you more positive with the driver and perhaps this is the ingredient you need for hitting the ball further from the tee? **(Figure 31)**

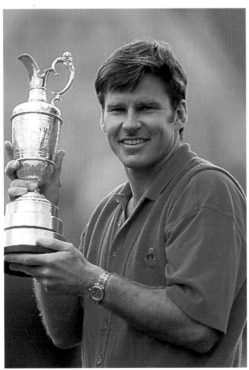

Figures 1 and 2: These two great players have given golfers throughout the world so much pleasure over the years. Both of them have shown on many occasions that, when the pressure is on, they know how to handle it. It has been said that great champions are separated from others by the way they think.

Figure 3: This challenge over the water at The Belfry helped to decide the outcome of three Ryder Cup competitions. There are times during a game of golf when we are offered an interesting challenge. All golfers should try to look upon so called difficult shots as interesting ones. This attitude will help to reduce the influence of fear and apprehension which are so often the cause of bad shots.

Figure 4: Costantino Rocca's rise to be a Ryder Cup star had a great deal to do with his near classical swing. His seemingly effortless method helps to produce good shots at critical times. All golfers, and in particular the young golfer, should try to use a swing which is tension free and not the white knuckle method which we so often see.

Figure 5: I am sure that we all appreciate the wise and knowledgeable comment of Peter Alliss. Much of his comment is based on the fact that he has "been there". He understands how golfers feel when they are under pressure. He also knows first hand that golf pressure can be very difficult to handle.

Figure 6: Much has been said about Bernhard Langer the golfer. As a man, it has to be said that he is as near the perfect gentleman as you can get. He is also known as a man who, through sheer grit and determination, overcame the problems of the short putt. His behaviour at all times is impeccable and this is just one of the reasons why, at this time, he leads the world of golf in tournament money earnings.

Figure 7: Throughout his career, Andrew Murray has had to deal with many health problems, but this never dampened his enthusiasm to play golf at such a high level. He has been an example over the years to his fellow professionals, as the man who never quits. Every player on Tour was delighted when he won the European Open.

Figure 8: Jack Nicklaus is still one of those players who is always there or there about when it comes to winning major tournaments. He has a record in Majors which may never be surpassed. Jack sets very high standards for himself and his determination to succeed increases with the importance of the occasion.

Figure 9: The secret of practice is to spend more time on the range when you are playing good golf. When you do have to analyze your swing to overcome a fault, please spend time with your professional so that you don't spend time practising your faults.

Figure 10: When you visit a Tour event you may be surprised to see just how much time the players spend on the practise ground after they have played. You may think, why do they do this, they already know how to play? Well they are looking to reinforce their confidence. They are not looking for some new magic move, just grooving the same swing to help play the pressure shot.

Figure 11: Whatever you practise you will become good at it. This will happen if you practice good or bad method. When you practice your putting you should spend most of your time playing from 3 feet from the hole. This is an exercise not just to make you feel good about those short putts, but knowing that you are good from short distances, will make the long ones so much easier.

Figure 12: Nick Price at Turnberry. The swing sequence of thoughts and the swing action should ideally take the same amount of time. Some players find that at crucial times they spend more time over the ball - this is not wise. If composure is required, it must take place prior to the swing sequence from a position away from the ball.

Figure 13: The first principle of target aiming is that we aim at a point. This principle is quite obvious when we realise that we can line-up better to a point than an area. Practise putting one ball up to another and you will be surprised how good you are.

Figure 14: Woosie and Wobbly deciding which club to take. It is not wise to assume that you know the distance of the shot you wish to play. Nor is it good planning to assume you know which line to take. Good course strategy saves shots. Make sure that you carry a course planner and have your landing areas marked on it.

Figure 15: Patience is a virtue in any walk of life. Some people are blessed with it, others must endeavour to find it. You may not wish to copy the way that Fuzzy Zoeller lines up his ball with the shaft of his club, but you could do no better than copy his laid-back approach to golf.

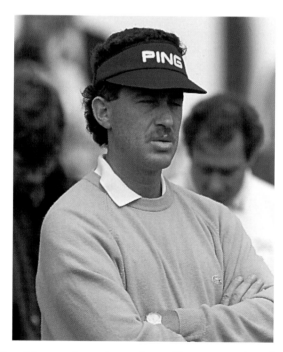

Figure 16: Miguel Angel Jimenez is another patient golfer. He goes about his business in a quiet and positive manner. When you go to a tournament and you want to watch quality golf, you could do no better than to follow Miguel.

Figure 17: What more can be said about this partnership? I'll bet that there have been many interesting stories passed between Arnold and Tip during the waiting times between shots. Passing the time with conversation which will distract you from worrying about the next shot is a relaxation technique which all golfers should follow.

Figure 18: Paul Way deep in the ferns on the 18th at Woburn. All golfers hit bad shots. How we play recovery shots relates to how often we practice them. You will feel much more confident about playing these shots if you accept that there are no difficult shots in golf. Some shots are simply more interesting than others.

Figure 19: Practising the inner game of golf requires that you use your imagination to watch someone play. Seve's smooth rhythmic action is one of the best to use. This method of learning is very powerful and all golfers should try to use it.

Figure 20: We have all heard the expression "practice makes perfect". There is only one way to improve your golf and that way is to practice. So many golfers only visit their course to play 18 holes and then wonder why they do not improve. Nothing happens on its own. You will only get return from effort.

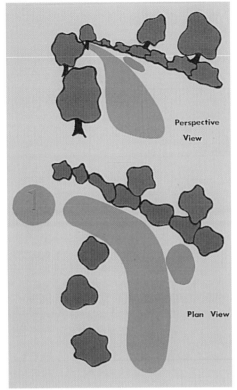

Figure 21: Perspective illusion. On a dog-leg hole the landing area can appear to be small.

Figure 22: The Muller-Lyer Illusion. The lines between the arrow heads are the same length.

Figures 21 and 22: These optical illusions should reinforce your belief in course management. The eye does deceive at times. If you are a serious golfer, you will not leaving anything to chance.

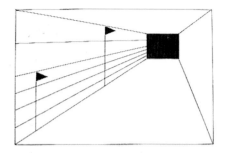

The two flags are the same height.

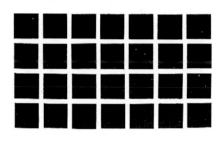

The grey areas between the black squares are not there.

Figure 23: Black and white squares

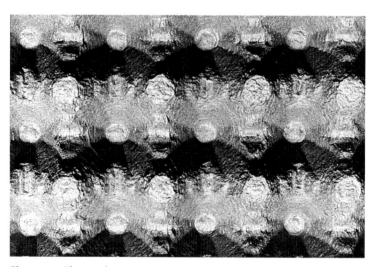

There are three sets of 'humps' in the egg box picture. Turn the book upside down and there are only two.

Figure 24: The egg box

Figures 23 and 24: Golf Architects design courses to make the golfer think. They position hazards to make the game more interesting. You should have a plan of action before you take up the challenge of any golf course.

Figure 25: The clubs which Fred Couples uses today are far removed from the ones he used when he started to play the game. Club design and technology has perhaps moved forwards more in the last decade than in the last century.

Figure 27: Greg Norman can generate so much spin on the ball that sometimes the ball spins back many yards after landing on the green. Club head speed is just one of the components in the ball spin mechanism.

Figure 26: The force applied to a golf ball in order to distort it from its round shape is extremely large. This photograph was taken by using a flash gun which fires for 1/3 of one millionth of one second. It has to be a fast flash because the ball is in contact with the club for only 1/2 of one thousandth of one second.

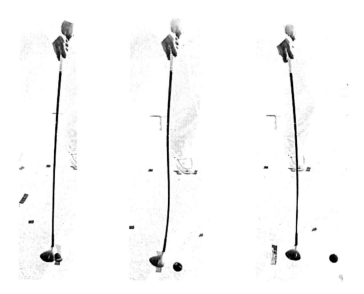

Figure 28: These photographs of the shaft through the impact period may surprise you, but they are real. The shaft shown is a dynamic gold R flex and it is me hitting the ball. What would the shaft be doing if Greg Norman had hit the ball?

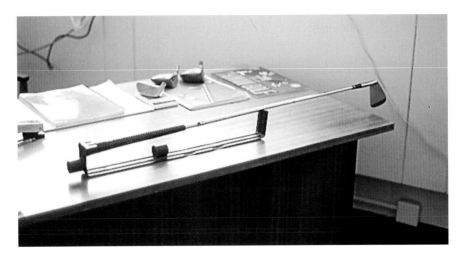

Figure 29: Swing weight is a manufacturers static measure. All clubs throughout a set are made to a scale number. In the past the most common swing weight number used was DO. Today we see numbers coming down - and not before time.

Figure 30: This little device helps to show golfers how the ball is influenced when the club twists during the ball and club contact time. Incidentally, the club and ball contact time is the same whether you use a driver or a putter. Time does change however for different types of ball.

Figure 31: Those of you who have had the pleasure of watching Seve play recovery shots can only applaud his skill. He is a master of all golf shots and none of it is down to luck. I sometimes think that when talent was issued, Seve got a double share.

Figure 32: All of us who are involved in this wonderful game of golf should feel privileged to spend so much of our time in such nice places. Our behaviour should reflect this privilege.

PREPARING TO PLAY

Preparation time for golf is a very exciting time. It is at this time when our ambitions are set and we dream of those fantastic scores which will ensure our victory. We imagine long putts dropping and long drives which split the fairways. We see ourselves being applauded by our fellow players, pointed out to strangers as the champion and being warmly welcomed wherever we go.

Well, in some ways this is all very good. It is this type of dream which provides the interest and enthusiasm to play. But preparing to play in a competition must start with a more realistic approach. We must realise and accept that our thinking must take into account that we cannot play beyond our capabilities. We all know what our limitations are and we must not wish to play at a level above our normal game. If we do ask for more than we can provide, then this "pressure by demand" can very quickly bring on the feelings of disappointment. Our enthusiasm to compete will then fall away very quickly.

There are those times when we do play better than our form suggests. But these are so infrequent and it is asking rather a lot for a good game to appear to order. We have all experienced those days when we have chipped in or had a lucky bounce, but these are rare occasions. Days do happen, when luck and everything else seems to go our way. But do not wish for one of these days to happen when preparing for competition. Wishful thinking will get you nowhere. It encourages the overwhelming urge to win and reduces the chances of playing anywhere near our personal best.

Our requirements for the day is the first priority. This preparation should be obvious and the condition of everything we need must compliment our intentions. We must also make every possible effort to look good, because to look good is to feel good. We should take care and make sure that at least we look as if we can play the game. This will be time well spent, because we will be practising the caring attitude which is very much a part of competition golf.

Golf is a game where good common sense reaps large rewards. One thing you should do is to sit down sometime when you have a few minutes to spare, and list all of your possible requirements. We all have special needs - may be a sticking plaster for a blistered finger or toe, perhaps a pack of indigestion tablets. All of these to help overcome the possibility of distracting thoughts entering our minds at times when we should be concentrating on our golf.

All of this pre golf preparation should be done well in advance of leaving for a tournament, but if it does help to avoid those night before nerves, do it then. And please remember to leave yourself time to "wind down" before going to bed.

As you know, a good night's sleep is essential if we are to be anything like efficient on the next day. So practise your relaxation techniques as soon as you get to bed, and even if you do not get to sleep quickly - after all you may not be tired - relax your body and then your mind and you will be storing the energy required for the next day.

Don't forget that the relaxation techniques used to provide those extra hours sleep need to be practised just as often as do other parts of your game. The more you practise relaxation the easier it will be to recall the feelings when they are required.

Just make sure that you do get a good night's sleep before a tournament, it really does help. You could be the best player in the world, but if you don't have the energy to win, then you'll be back in the pack. Golf is not just about hitting a golf ball it's about the whole package from the start of preparation to the prize giving. You must get the whole thing right.

If the day and evening before are properly organized then the morning should start with the peace of mind that everything is ready for the journey to the course. During this journey try not to allow a traffic problem to "wind you up". There are plenty of fools who drive cars these days and they can put you in situations which could tax your patience. Leaving home in plenty of time can help overcome this problem but remember that it is just as easy to smile about inconsiderate drivers as it is to fly into a rage.

Starting times can sometimes be awkward and we must allow time to adjust. Driving to the course after breakfast and having just enough time to prepare before teeing off is perhaps the ideal arrangement for most players. This is particularly true if you are a morning person. But if you do have a late time please do not use up too much nervous energy. Try not to allow yourself to get too excited about the forthcoming competition. Play it cool and enjoy the day.

There is one particular thing which you should avoid doing during this time, and on the days running up to a competition. You must avoid hitting golf balls just for the sake of something to do. We often see golfers following this habit and they must understand that it is not always positive. You should never hit golf balls to pass the time unless you are prepared to practise sensibly. Always hit balls following your swing sequence with the full concentration to play any shot. Do it right and you will practise successfully, do it wrong and you will practise failure.

The routine to follow when you arrive at the course should be quite straight forward. Try to be as normal with your routine as you possibly can be, although we all know that competition changes our attitude to some degree. We have to cope with added pressure, but don't be too concerned. It is important not to try and remove all of the extra excitement because this ensures that we can offer a little extra care where care is needed. The important thing to remember is that we must not race about, either physically or mentally. If you can keep calm it will help achieve the ideal mood in which to play.

Booking-in is an extra thing to do, so get it out of the way as soon as you can. It's another one of those positive things to do; it removes the possibility of another worrying thought which might go through your mind. Try to occupy your mind with pleasant thoughts by associating with your friends until it is time to "get ready".

The players on the European Tour, start their warm-up session, one hour before their tee-up time. This has proved over the years to be an ideal time schedule for them, so it's not a bad system to follow. How much time you are prepared to give to practise is your concern, but just make sure that you are ready to play. If you are serious, then do not leave things to chance.

If the course that you are about to challenge has the facility to practise, then you should at least hit a few balls to get the system warmed up. Our swing is often slightly different from day to day, so find out how it is performing.

Start with a few short wedge shots and finish with your favourite club. You do not have to go through the whole bag, and remember to only allow yourself a positive amount of time to practise. Stay there too long and you may start to get it wrong. Practise only the shots which you can play well. Time spent playing shots with your favourite club will provide confidence and remind your automatic swing of the "tempo" you require. If you do have a particular club which you have not been playing well of late, leave it in the car. This is not the time to practise failure. Pre competition practise time is an ego boosting time, a time for reward, just make sure that you make the most of it.

Notes

An understanding of how our game is today also applies to the putter and time must always be spent on this exacting part of your game. If ever you are short of warm-up time then use the available time on the putting green and a little time for stretching exercises on the first tee. Never be afraid of being seen doing these exercises on the first tee. People won't think that you are being silly: on the contrary, they will know you mean business.

Your work on the putting surface must again be constructive. Don't be there because everybody else is, use the time wisely. A few long ones to feel the distance and a lot of those short ones. Try not to practise missing - get close enough to get them all in. This is a time to produce the feelings of confidence so go about your business sensibly.

The only thing left before we go to the tee is to remind ourselves just "why we are here". Find a quiet place - your car is an ideal place - but if it is not close at hand, move away and stand somewhere on your own. Tell yourself that the first reason of playing in this competition is to win, and if at any time this possibility becomes remote, then you will replace it with something else to make sure that you keep on trying until the game is over. You will play for your own personal achievement and beat yourself - not the other competitors - and then you will have a good chance of winning. Remember to leave out the aggressive approach and hit the ball with controlled authority. Remind yourself that you will remain patient with yourself and tolerant of others; that you will adhere to your course plan, and that above all else you will smile and be happy. REMEMBER AGAIN - THERE ARE NO DIFFICULT SHOTS IN THE GAME OF GOLF, SOME SHOTS ARE SIMPLY MORE INTERESTING THAN OTHERS.

THE LEARNING PROGRAMME

The learning programme is designed to be simple and not to give the impression that it is difficult to learn the lessons of the golfing mind. Each lesson will be simple and easy, thus allowing small changes to be made in your normal game. This slight change of behaviour will stop that depressing falling off in performance which can often happen when making physical alterations to your swing.

There are only six short lessons and they are the basis of learning how to become a more consistent golfer. You must practise these simple methods of relaxation, concentration and preparation, until they become part of your automatic game. At all times you must enjoy your practise, making sure that you are not practising bad technique or poor mental attitude.

From young to old, we are constantly looking for ways to improve our standard at this very demanding game. Work on these lessons of the mind - particularly relaxation - it will improve your play and the quality of your everyday life.

LESSON ONE

RELAXATION

Understandably our first lesson should start with practising relaxation and the diaphragm breathing technique. It is a simple procedure which we have already discussed and it should first be practised from the "sitting comfortably" position. When out on the golf course you can try relaxing over the ball by breathing out before starting your backswing.

Learning to relax in the sitting comfortable position is a very pleasant way to spend your time; you will feel the benefits immediately because these exercises produce a feeling of calm in your body. How do you know if you are doing it correctly? Well, heavy is the feeling that you are looking for - heavy arms, hands and legs, with a faint feeling of "pins and needles" in your fingers. The periods of time that you set aside for these exercises should be any time between two and twenty minutes with the best times for the longer sessions being just before sleep.

Relaxation must become second nature. Practise until it becomes engrained into your behaviour and always remember that to keep calm is almost relaxation and will help to reduce the pressure which makes relaxation necessary. The more you practise, the easier it will become to find the feelings of peace needed to avoid pressure.

LESSON TWO

THE TARGET

Target aiming is at a point: drive at a point, chip at a point and, very importantly, putt at a point. Common sense tells us that we cannot line-up to an area.

Target aiming and concentration are very much connected. Your target aiming ritual should follow a series of thoughts and movements called "concentration steps." These should be used for every shot from your drive to your putt. I would suggest that you should have 5 or 6 steps, two of which should be swing instructions. When the pressure is on and the mind becomes difficult to organise one thought at the beginning of the backswing and one at the beginning of the downswing are quite enough to cope with at that time.

Of course this ritual should be practised inside your "personal bubble". This will help to avoid distraction, and remember, if you do need to compose yourself, do this before starting your aiming ritual.

When organising your concentration steps please remember that you should try not to involve more thoughts than you can manage on competition day. Swing thoughts on the practise ground can be quite numerous but in the heat of competition things happen differently and we must make allowances.

LESSON THREE

COURSE STRATEGY

To be confident at golf you have to make the right decisions. One way we can do this is to remove the doubt about the line and length of all shots. Planning "fairway greens" is not a difficult thing to do, but it may require more than one practise round.

You must be sure that the position you seek on the fairway gives you

the best line into the green for your type of game. If you "shape" the ball right to left then you may require a different fairway position to someone who shapes the ball the other way. This type of information gives the practise round more interest, and please do not let your ambition to score well override the objectives of the practise round. Another reason for the practise round is to find the layout of each

green. We need to know the slope of each green and if they vary in pace from the greens we play on our home course.

Setting out course strategy is an exercise in common sense. There is

not too much information to gather but it is important information. We must understand the best way to solve the problems placed before us by the golf course architect, then we can set about beating the course, ourselves, and the opposition.

LESSON FOUR

POSITIVE PRACTISE

All practice sessions should provide reward. Without reward, it is difficult to find the time. The most effective time to be on the range is when you are in control of your game. You are then practising in a positive manner. Do not forget that you should practice playing recovery shots.

Do not take too many balls to the practice range. This will ensure that you do not spend too much time without a break and get to the stage when things start to go wrong.

If you have to sort out a swing fault, please do so under the instruction of your teaching professional. Do not practice faults.

Take enough balls to the practice putting green to fill the hole. Most of your work must be from three feet, the occasional long ones are OK - but not too many.

Positive practise lies not in how much time you spend there, but in using your time wisely.

LESSON FIVE

PRESSURE GOLF

There is a golden rule as far as pressure is concerned and it says that we must take steps to avoid pressure rather than just knowing how to cope with it. To be in control of our thoughts and actions -as we must when playing golf - is the result of good preparation, an appreciation of our own limitations and of course a knowledge of relaxation.

The main thing to remember, is that you are just as capable to hit bad shots and find bad lies as anyone. If you can allow for this as being a part of golf, then you will perform to a much higher standard. Do not allow yourself to become negative by protecting your score or by becoming too complacent and never ever give-in.

Pressure in most cases is self-inflicted by the placing of demands on yourself. Like I must make a birdie here, or this putt must go in. These are negative thoughts and will only make things worse. Making birdies and holing putts come from good golf, not by demand.

You must stay calm and relaxed before and during a competition and not use up your store of energy required to complete the job. You and only you are responsible for overcoming the pressures you find at golf.

LESSON SIX

PREPARING FOR COMPETITION

Lesson Six has three objectives and they are:-

-   to make you feel good before each game.

-   to know that you have catered for all of your needs - which will reduce anxiety.

-   to know that you look presentable and are in control.

Preparing to play golf is much more than gathering together all the equipment for the day. During this time you should be starting to develop the pleasant mood needed for golf. Be meticulous when cleaning your shoes, clubs and bag and be concerned about the clothes you wear both on and off the course. To look good is to feel good but we are really seeking that "caring" mood which helps provide good concentration.

Design a practise range routine for competition day. It should be not much more than hitting golf balls with your favourite club. At this time we need to remind our automatic self of "tempo" and boost our confidence by seeing and feeling good golf shots.

Use your time wisely on the putting surface. Don't spend your time missing putts and hoping that when the competition starts the putts will start to drop. Get close enough to the hole to hole all of your putts. When you reach the first green you must feel good about your putting.

Please take your smile to golf and golf will smile back at you.

IN CONCLUSION

Figure 32: Wollaton Park - Such a lovely
place to spend your time

Please remember what the game of golf is all about. Yes, it is about hitting golf balls and winning tournaments, but it is much more than this. It's about friendships, a relationship with the countryside, the comradeship of the friendly fourball, travelling and meeting people.

The game of golf offers the golfer so much, please remember to show it the respect it deserves. If you are to benefit from the privilege of being part of the great game of golf you have to be patient with yourself, be tolerant of others, be scrupulously honest, and at all times behave like ladies and gentlemen.

Golf has always been a game for ladies and gentlemen. As Arnold Palmer might say, "Let's keep it that way."